Welcome to the EVERYTHING® series!

THESE HANDY, accessible books give you all you need to tackle a difficult project, gain a new hobby, comprehend a fascinating topic, prepare for an exam, or even brush up on something you learned back in school but have since forgotten.

You can read an *EVERYTHING*® book from cover to cover or just pick out the information you want from our four useful boxes: e-facts, e-ssentials, e-alerts, and e-questions. We literally give you everything you need to know on the subject, but throw in a lot of fun stuff along the way, too.

We now have well over 100 *EVERYTHING*® books in print, spanning such wide-ranging topics as weddings, pregnancy, wine, learning guitar, one-pot cooking, managing people, and so much more. When you're done reading them all, you can finally say you know *EVERYTHING*®!

Ⓔ **FACTS:** Important sound bytes of information

Ⓔ **ESSENTIALS:** Quick and handy tips

Ⓔ **ALERTS!:** Urgent warnings

Ⓔ **QUESTIONS?:** Solutions to common problems

THE EVERYTHING Series

Dear Reader,

Parents around the world begin potty training infants and babies using gentle, compassionate methods geared to their development. Meanwhile, the customary age for starting potty training in the United States has been continually delayed. Now, when training begins just as toddlers are starting to assert their independence, deeper issues often surface. Too often, potty training becomes a source of frustration and conflict instead of a time for teaching and learning.

When their child's potty training stalls, parents must realize that although they can coach and encourage, they cannot control their child. Toddlers are full-fledged people with minds and wills of their own. When parents can accept this sometimes difficult reality, they open the door to a healthier relationship. Then, the challenges of the training process pale in comparison to the deeper pleasure they derive from parenting.

As your guide on this leg of your parenting journey, I urge you to be patient with yourself as well as your youngster. How long it takes a child to reach the final potty training destination doesn't matter—every normal child eventually arrives. If, in the process, you learn to serve as your child's teacher, coach, and cheerleader, far greater treasures will be yours. And those treasures will last a lifetime.

Sincerely,

Dr. Lsomm

THE
EVERYTHING
POTTY
TRAINING
BOOK

Professional, reassuring advice
to help you and your child
through this challenging time

Linda Sonna, Ph.D.

Adams Media Corporation
Avon, Massachusetts

An Everything® Series Book.
Everything® and everything.com® are registered trademarks of
Adams Media Corporation.

Published by Adams Media Corporation
57 Littlefield Street, Avon, MA 02322 U.S.A.
www.adamsmedia.com

ISBN: 1-58062-740-4
Printed in Canada.

J   I   H   G   F   E   D   C   B

Library of Congress Cataloging-in-Publication Data
Sonna, Linda.
The everything potty training book / Linda Sonna.
   p.   cm. — (An everything series book)
Includes bibliographical references and index.
ISBN 1-58062-740-4
1. Toilet training. I. Title. II. Everything series.
HQ770.5 .S66 2003
649'.62—dc21
2002009828

This publication is designed to provide accurate and authoritative information with regard to the subject matter covered. It is sold with the understanding that the publisher is not engaged in rendering legal, accounting,
or other professional advice. If legal advice or other expert assistance is
required, the services of a competent professional person should be sought.
         —From a *Declaration of Principles* jointly adopted by a
                  Committee of the American Bar Association and
                        a Committee of Publishers and Associations

Illustrations by Barry Littmann.

This book is available at quantity discounts for bulk purchases.
For information, call 1-800-872-5627.

Visit the entire Everything® series at everything.com

THE

EVERYTHING
Series

EDITORIAL

Publishing Director: Gary M. Krebs
Managing Editor: Kate McBride
Copy Chief: Laura MacLaughlin
Acquisitions Editors: Allison Carpenter Yoder
and Bethany Brown
Development Editor: Christel A. Shea
Production Editor: Khrysti Nazzaro

PRODUCTION

Production Director: Susan Beale
Production Manager: Michelle Roy Kelly
Series Designer: Daria Perreault
Cover Design: Paul Beatrice and Frank Rivera
Layout and Graphics: Colleen Cunningham,
Rachael Eiben, Michelle Roy Kelly,
Daria Perreault, Erin Ring

Contents

Dedication

To Margie Henzel of *Positive Parenting Magazine*.

Acknowledgments

Thanks to Brandy Corry, Laurie Boucke, Lois Mark, and Mary Gugino for their help with this book.

Introduction

THE FIRST THING PARENTS WANT to know about potty training is when they should begin. Of all the questions parents ask on the subject, that one is the easiest to answer: The time to begin is now!

Repetition is the name of the game! Just as infants and babies quickly learn that milk comes from a breast or bottle and that parents respond to their smiles with joy and their tears by giving comfort, they can learn concepts and routines and engage in a variety of early learning experiences that simplify and speed later training. They can enjoy sitting on the potty and can come to accept it as one of their normal routines.

If toddlers have no prior experience with elimination and potties, they have lots to learn. Actually, since they've been wetting and soiling in diapers for years, they have lots to unlearn! Nevertheless, potty training older children usually turns out to be far less demanding than parents anticipate.

Starting Early

In most cultures of the world parents catch infant's waste in a small pot or hold them over a patch of ground instead of putting them in diapers. (Parents in the United States did the same until around 1940.)

Where diaper use is minimal or nonexistent, families learn infants' rhythms and respond quickly to prevent messy accidents. Some say the parents are trained, not the children. In some ways this is true. Yet little ones come to recognize the physical sensations that precede elimination and learn where to relieve themselves. Many such infants begin signaling when they need their little potty bowl. Even if diapers are used some of the time, wetting and soiling are less likely to become such entrenched habits. Because this age-old approach to dealing with infants promotes parent/child bonding, prevents diaper rash, is better for the environment, and is far more hygienic, more and more North American parents are placing their children on the infant and baby training tracks.

Toddler Training

Older toddlers can master the necessary vocabulary, concepts, and basic skills needed for potty training in short order. Common sticking points are difficulties identifying sensations, learning to control their muscles, and overcoming the habit of wetting and soiling in diapers. The fast-track method wherein parents provide intensive, concentrated instruction to two-year-olds during the course of a single day works like a charm for many families, but it is definitely not for everyone. Many adults find this method overly challenging or feel that it conflicts with their basic beliefs about childrearing.

Most pediatricians, including T. Berry Brazelton, who wrote the American Academy of Pediatrics guidelines, recommend the popular potties-without-pressure method. Parents may wait to introduce the potty until age thirty to thirty-six months for girls, and shortly after the third birthday for boys, unless a child expresses interest in learning sooner. Parents reward successes, and are careful not to punish or create shame about accidents. Instead, they work to instill confidence as youngsters set out to learn a set of new procedures they may find mystifying. When they master them and join the ranks of the "big" boys and girls, they can take pride in their increased independence.

Then, when the story reaches its inevitable happy conclusion, parents and children can join hands and walk blissfully into the sunset—and for once, they can leave the diaper bag behind.

CHAPTER 1
The Potty Coach

Maybe this is your first time as a potty trainer, and you need to know where to begin. Or, maybe this is not your first time, but you are still looking for a method that works better for your situation. Before you start choosing methods, get comfortable with what the job ahead entails for you and your family. Patience, flexibility, and compassion are essential.

Meet Jenna and Tod

Like many first-time mothers, Jenna was uncertain how to go about potty training her son. After talking to friends and relatives and reading some articles on the subject, she was sure her twenty-eight-month-old had sufficient bladder and bowel control to be trained, and since Tod disliked having his diapers changed, he might gladly give them up. She took him to the store so he could help pick out a potty chair, bought a storybook on the subject, and purchased some stickers to use as rewards. Back at home, she promised that he could wear his new "big boy" underpants whenever he wanted to try the potty. Then she waited for Tod to signal interest. When a week went by and he still hadn't shown any interest, she decided it was time for a nudge.

Ⓔ ESSENTIAL

A child must see himself eliminating to grasp that waste comes from his own body. Find a place where accidents won't do too much damage, remove your child's diaper, and when he begins relieving himself, point it out.

She read him the storybook again, and explained that Tod would soon use the potty just like the main character. It was summertime, so Jenna took off Tod's clothes and suggested he have some fun sprinkling the flowers out back. Then she explained that inside the house, he should go pee-pee in his little potty. After dinner that night he approached her and said, "Pee-pee." She walked him to the bathroom, helped him undress, and he urinated in the potty. "Way to go!" she exclaimed as she handed him a sticker and helped him don his "big boy" pants. She thought she was home clear—and she was!

Tod did have an occasional nighttime accident and a two-week setback when his baby brother was born, but overall, Tod managed the potty like a trooper. Jenna had a hard time relating to the troubles many of her friends recounted. It seemed to her that if children were physically ready, children basically trained themselves.

Parents as Partners

Although it's true that potty training often proceeds with remarkable ease, Jenna's contribution was far more important than she realized. She did her homework before beginning. She established that Tod had the wherewithal to control his bladder and bowel. She involved him in the process by letting him help choose the potty chair. She explained the procedures using a storybook. She offered the incentive of "big boy" pants and gave stickers as tangible rewards. When she took off his diapers and let him urinate outside, she made sure he grasped the all-important concept that urine came from his own body. Furthermore, Jenna didn't pressure Tod to perform. She gently praised his successes and didn't overreact when he had accidents.

Potty Training Problems

Tod was exceptionally easy to potty train, but Jenna soon discovered how very difficult this process can be when a child isn't ready.

Jenna expected her youngest son to be even easier to potty train. Jacob idolized his big brother and liked to do whatever Tod did. By the time he was twenty months old Jacob would occasionally follow Tod into the bathroom and urinate in the regular toilet alongside him. When she was seven months pregnant with her third child, Jenna felt it important to have Jacob potty trained before the next baby arrived. Things started to bog down almost immediately.

The "Trained" Parent

If Jenna caught Jacob at the right moment and took him to the toilet, he would use it. But try as she might, she couldn't get him to tell her when he needed to go. That meant several accidents each day. She tried incentives and rewards, storybooks and stickers, but nothing sparked his interest.

One day when Jenna heard him grunting, she swooped him up despite his protests and ran him to the bathroom. He held it in until she let him get off the potty. A few minutes later he messed in his pants. "You're supposed to go in the potty!" she said sharply. Jacob looked repentant, but the next time she tried to take him to the bathroom, he threw a tantrum. She ended up sending him to time-out, and he messed in his pants.

 ALERT!

New underpants and a new challenge generate motivation at the outset of potty training, but enthusiasm may fade when children realize they must drop whatever they are doing when nature calls. Give your child consistent attention and encouragement until the habit forms.

Jenna tried to remain calm when Jacob refused to go near the potty over the next weeks, but she was tired of diapers and her advanced pregnancy was making her cranky. She began putting him on the potty at regular intervals, entertaining him by reading books and singing songs about potties. Sometimes he urinated during that time. More often he wet his pants shortly afterward.

Constipation became an increasingly serious problem. Jacob would go for days without having a bowel movement, then scream in pain when he tried. The pediatrician prescribed enemas and laxatives to relieve the hard, painful bowel movements, but they didn't cure the bigger problem. It got to the point that when Jenna so much as mentioned the potty, Jacob would cloak himself in silence, refusing to respond to her inquiries, explanations, and entreaties.

Jacob was still in diapers when he started kindergarten. If he was upset about being teased, he kept his feelings to himself. The chronic soiling and frequent wetting continued.

Finally Jenna determined that she had done everything in her power to help him. She placed the ball squarely in Jacob's court, trusting that sooner or later he'd pick it up and run with it. Six months went by before he did.

Ending Power Struggles

Jenna learned the hard way that when a parent and child end up in power struggles over the potty, the child wins every time, and that means that everyone loses. The bottom line is that children's bodies are their own. A child's elimination is an intimate matter, and beyond anyone else's control.

Jacob's early imitation of his big brother had convinced Jenna that he was ready to be fully trained, but occasionally following a big brother into the bathroom for fun is one thing; going to the potty when there are other, more interesting things to do is quite another. Jacob might have been physically ready, but he wasn't emotionally ready to handle so much responsibility. Jenna's advanced pregnancy sapped the energy and patience she needed to give the project her all.

Jacob's resistance hardened in the face of the pressure Jenna placed on him to perform. Soon he was in too much turmoil to hear the signals his own body was sending him, hazed as his mind was by anxiety. Even after his mother backed off, he needed time to heal emotionally before he could move forward.

Ⓔ **ALERT!**

Don't start potty training when you are busy or stressed. Choose a period of relative calm so you can remain patient and devote yourself fully to the task. Picking the right time will help ensure a relaxed and successful experience for both of you.

Jenna's advice to other parents is as emphatic as it is sound. "If your child isn't ready, back off!" However, Jenna would have been wise to add the following bit of advice to parents. "If you find yourself in over your head, back off!"

Know When to Stop

It makes no sense to keep battling to get a car up a hill when the engine has stalled and you don't know what's wrong or how to fix it. If you lift the hood and begin pounding the engine with a hammer, you will do more harm than good. Doggedly turning the starter will probably only drain your car's battery. Pushing the car uphill requires a Herculean effort that is unlikely to solve anything anyway. In such a situation, you need to contain yourself and refrain from reacting until you can think clearly and decide how best to proceed. In the meantime, it's always possible to go back to walking. However loath you may be to do so, that action may require less energy in the long run. In the case of potty training, that means putting the project on hold and returning to diapers for a month or two.

Parents as Potty Coaches

Potty training is a straightforward process. If you feel nervous, it may be because the very word "training" conjures images of housebreaking a pet. Most people don't know how to teach puppies and kittens that the house is not a giant litterbox, so they end up using some pretty heavyhanded techniques on the poor Fidos of the world. For this reason, many parenting experts want to eliminate the phrase "potty training" altogether. For infants and babies, it *is* potty training, except the parent is more trained than the child! For toddlers it is "potty learning." Your job will be to serve as coach to work out a game plan and supervise practice sessions, as a teacher to provide instruction, and as a cheerleader to nurture a can-do attitude.

Your Role as Coach

Potty coaches recognize that little athletes need to be well-rested, physically up to par, and emotionally ready to tackle a new skill. If your baby is ill, put her back in diapers. If your toddler is under the weather or preoccupied with other problems, let her choose whether she wants to wear diapers or underpants. While wearing diapers she can practice a skill she has already mastered, such as checking from time to time to see if she needs a diaper change. That way, she continues to work on learning the difference between wet and dry, but doesn't constantly have to worry about the potty.

Ⓔ ALERT!

> If an ill toddler refuses diapers and insists on wearing pull-ups or underpants when she has diarrhea or a bladder infection, try putting a waterproof diaper cover over them. That will lessen the mess and permit her to go to the potty by herself if she wishes.

Coaches also know the importance of standing back and allowing children to struggle on their own. Too much hands-on help deprives them of the opportunity to learn. Too many verbal pointers distract them. On the other hand, coaches must not expect their young charges to do more than they can handle on their own. Otherwise, they become overwhelmed by the frustration of accidents. Pointing out when your child needs to use the potty and giving occasional reminders may be very important until she is better at remembering on her own.

Positive Practice

Coaches also know that when it comes to practice, more is not necessarily better. Conscientious toddlers may end up constantly worrying about having an accident. Too much concentration on toilet training leads to burnout. Sometimes the best course is to put the whole subject out of both your minds for a time. There is more to life than potties!

⒠ ESSENTIAL

> If you assign a task that is too hard, follow up with something easy and fun for your child, such as running to the potty, sitting down for two seconds, and jumping back up. Learning to get to the potty fast is important!

Good coaches also try to ensure that each learning session ends on a positive note. Always express confidence that your child will learn in time. Pointing out how much he has mastered thus far prevents both of you from becoming discouraged.

Teacher Talk

Are you wondering how to communicate with babies and toddlers who don't understand much of what you say, and don't speak very well, if at all? Fortunately, youngsters understand more than they can verbalize. Still, you must take special steps to facilitate comprehension.

Get your child's full attention before speaking. If you tell your child to go to the potty and get no response, she may not have even realized that you were speaking to her. Always begin by saying your child's name. Don't continue until she looks up.

Tell your child what to do rather than what not to do. Sentences containing negative words (such as "don't") are hard to grasp. To comprehend "don't stand up," children must understand "stand up," and then understand that "don't" means they are to do the opposite. That's too confusing! "Sit down" is much clearer.

Combine words with gestures. Point to the bathroom when you tell your child to go there. Pat the potty when telling him to sit down on the potty. Children learn by hearing words combined with visual signals.

Use consistent language. It's hard enough for a youngster to learn, "Go to the potty." He may not also understand, "Let mama take you to the bathroom," "Come with me to the potty," "Let's take you to the potty," "Let's get you into the toilet fast." Choose a single set of words and phrases, and stick to them!

Show toddlers exactly what to do. Put a stuffed animal on the potty. Enlist a willing sibling or parent to give a demonstration, or use a doll that wets. Read storybooks about potties.

Combine verbal instructions with manual guidance. Place your hands on your child's shoulders and apply gentle pressure while telling him to sit on the potty. Cover his hands with yours to help him remove his pants. Show him what to do while you tell him.

Combining verbal, visual, and physical direction helps children learn new vocabulary and enhances communication. To be a good teacher, use every means at your disposal to help your little student understand what he's to do!

Little Lessons

Good teachers break big tasks into a series of small steps and present them one at a time so as not to overwhelm young learners. The mere act of sitting down on a potty seems simple enough to adults, but the unfamiliar feel of a seat with a hole in the middle and the sensation of cold, hard plastic on a soft, warm bottom can be hard to handle! Break even this simple task into smaller steps.

(E) ALERT!

If your child carries the potty around the house and plays with it as well as using it to relieve herself, spray it with a mixture of one part bleach to nine parts water and wipe it with a clean cloth to sterilize it.

Let the new potty sit in the bathroom for several days so your child becomes accustomed to seeing it. Let her carry it around the house and play with it in her own way. Unless she can't wait to try it, have her sit on it fully clothed several times before trying it bare-bottomed. That way, she can adjust to sitting low to the ground on a chair with a hole in the middle before experiencing the cold seat. It's better to move too slowly than too fast!

Providing Feedback

To coach effectively, you need to give children lots of feedback to help them understand what is happening. There are three kinds of feedback.

1. Neutral feedback is a straightforward statement that gives youngsters information about what they are doing, for example, "You're urinating." This kind of basic information is important for children who have always worn diapers and don't even realize when they are passing waste.
2. Positive feedback informs students about what they are doing correctly so they know to repeat it, for example, "Good! You're urinating in the potty!"
3. Negative feedback tells them what they are doing wrong, as in "Oh, no! You're urinating in your pants!" If you do give negative feedback, be sure to tell your child how to correct the mistake: "Oh no! You're urinating in your pants! You need to do that in the potty!"

Some toddlers are bolder and more confident than others. They may not learn anything from negative feedback, but they aren't especially daunted by it, either. Other children are far more sensitive. Even a hint that they are doing something wrong destroys their confidence, and they give up. They need lots of positive feedback to stay motivated!

Warm Fuzzies and Cold Pricklies

If a mother instructs a child to sit on the potty and the child stays there for two seconds before jumping up, the parent has a choice. She can give neutral feedback by describing exactly what the child did, "You sat on the potty and then you stood up." She can give negative feedback to let him know he blew it, "No! Come back here. I told you to sit down!" This can confuse and overwhelm the child who in fact followed the directions by sitting, if only very briefly. Another option is to give positive feedback to let the child know he succeeded: "Great job! You sat on the potty!"

Giving positive feedback has been likened to handing out warm fuzzies because acknowledging a child's accomplishments is a wonderful gift. Giving negative feedback has been likened to bestowing cold pricklies because a child feels criticized. When parents focus on a child's errors, mistakes, and omissions, the child may become convinced that, try as she might, she can't get things right. Many children stop listening altogether and tune their parents out to the point that some worry that their youngsters have hearing problems. Other children adopt an I-don't-care attitude to defend against repeated blows to their egos. If your child seems never to listen to you, the problem may be that he has listened too well and taken your many negative comments too much to heart!

(E) ESSENTIAL

> Don't blame your child if he doesn't appear to be learning. Instead of giving negative feedback, focus on every little thing your child does right! Let him know he can please you, and that he can succeed.

If your child doesn't even attempt to sit on the potty when instructed, set him up to succeed and then give positive feedback instead of criticizing. For instance, place a Teddy bear on the potty and praise it. Ask your child to pat the bear's head, and praise your child if he does by saying, "Yes! Teddy likes that!"

Praise and Pressure

Praise is a type of positive feedback that communicates, "I am proud that you did that." Praise can help children feel good about themselves, build confidence, and motivate them to repeat certain behaviors. However, when toddlers are grappling with independence issues, they sometimes feel compelled to do the exact opposite of what parents want. They may take strong exception to praise. Instead of gushing, "You used the potty! Mommy's so proud of you" offhand comments such as, "Aren't you proud of yourself?" or "You should be proud" can be more effective.

Motivational Tools

Two main psychological tools increase motivation. Positive reinforcement involves giving the child something she likes, such as hugs, toys, treats, or praise. Negative reinforcement enables the child to escape or avoid something unpleasant, such as escaping dirty diapers or avoiding upset parents because she uses the potty. Positive reinforcement is far more effective than negative reinforcement.

 ALERT!

Threats or punishment during potty training can backfire dramatically. Fear mobilizes children's inborn fight-or-flight impulse. The child may not fight back or flee at the time, but will start avoiding the potty, and his aggressive behavior toward siblings, peers, pets, parents, or caregivers may increase.

Many parents don't know when they have provoked their child's flight response. When a youngster says that she doesn't need to use the potty, her parents may think she is lying. They may not realize that fear propelled her to try to avoid going potty. Children may flee psychologically by ignoring all thoughts about elimination to the point that they tune out their bodies and don't realize they need to relieve themselves, although their parents may see the signs very clearly. Some youngsters struggle with themselves, unable to relax and let go so much so that they can't urinate for many hours at a stretch, even as they are screaming in pain from an overly full bladder. Others withhold stool, becoming constipated or even encopretic—a condition resulting in chronic, uncontrollable soiling. Initially very painful, the nerve endings soon become numb so children feel nothing. It's easy to see why experts' number one potty training rule is never to punish!

Negative Reinforcement

Having pants stay clean, dry, and odor-free motivates youngsters who dislike wet, messy pants, but most children don't mind them. In fact, many are quite attached to their diapers, wet or dry, smelly or not. In general, children have no natural aversion to waste. They love to smear, mash, pat, and taste. This behavior is normal, but can make them very sick, so supervise carefully.

Your Commitment

Rewards must be sufficiently enjoyable to outweigh children's reluctance to go to the potty. Pleasing a parent matters lots to most children, so hugs and kisses and other expressions of approval may keep them motivated. Spending one-on-one time with you will feel like a great reward, so when you accompany your youngster to the bathroom and serve as an attentive audience, your presence can provide a powerful incentive.

ⒺQUESTION?

Could my child be having accidents just to spite me?
Purposeful "accidents" may be a way to get attention. Even negative parental attention feels better to most children than being ignored. Try being matter-of-fact about accidents, and give lots of positive attention if your child so much as goes near the potty.

Problems motivating children often coincide with flagging parental motivation. Because parents feel disinclined to run to the bathroom each time their toddler beckons, they begin foot dragging in hopes their youngster's desire for company can be forestalled. To stay motivated, parents should remember that they can either drop what they're doing right now and fulfill their child's request for company in the bathroom, or drop what they're doing in a few minutes and spend time cleaning up an accident.

Sometimes stickers, small toys, treats, or special privileges can reduce demands on parents' time. Providing tangible evidence of the child's accomplishment can help instill pride in a job well done, and by doling out rewards, parents remain involved without having to spend so much time sitting in the bathroom with their child. However, some experts point out that playing into toddler greed and giving prizes instead of attention warps children's values. A preprinted smiley face is no substitute for a parent's smiling face. If you give treats and toys, it's important to give positive attention, too.

Ⓔ ESSENTIAL

Reward potty progress with a special phone call to Grandma Lois, Uncle Mark, Cousin David, or any family friend willing to "ooh" and "ah" over the latest victory. Put your child on the line, or be sure she listens in as you share the good news. This means a lot to little folks.

Effective Rewards

Anyone who has ever tried to diet knows how difficult it is to practice self-denial today to reap a reward in a month or two. Therefore, a good reward is something your child can enjoy immediately. Promises of a chance to put a quarter in a grocery store gumball machine tomorrow, to hear an extra bedtime story later in the evening, or to receive a special toy in a week do not motivate most children. It's more effective to offer an on-the-spot hug, sticker, or story.

Modeling

Children relish doing what friends and other family members do. If toddlers regularly see parents using the toilet, they are likely to want to copy them. Saying that using the potty makes them a "big girl" or a "big boy" just like an idolized parent, or older sibling, friend, or relative can motivate them!

Modeling is the most potent form of teaching. Having a coach explain how to dribble a ball isn't nearly as effective as having him demonstrate. Because children attending day care centers have many opportunities to observe and mimic more accomplished peers, they often master potty training earlier than stay-at-home peers. Similarly, younger siblings learn more quickly if older brothers, sisters, and/or parents allow them to watch. Let your child watch you use the bathroom or find someone else who is willing to serve as a model.

Unfortunately, the prospect of becoming a big boy or girl doesn't always strike toddlers as appealing. While little folks sometimes enjoy the greater freedom, independence, autonomy, and respect that come with using the potty, at other times they grasp the downside—they are saddled with big responsibilities. Big people do less for them and expect them to do more for themselves. In fact, the pressures for increased maturity inherent in potty training often cause children to stop progressing or to regress in other areas. Parents can help toddlers overcome their ambivalence about growing up by reducing demands in other areas, tolerating more clinging, and providing extra doses of TLC.

Anger Management for Potty Trainers

For many parents, potty training triggers a host of fears ("Will my child ever learn?"), feelings of inadequacy ("I must be doing something wrong"), insecurity ("Other children her age are trained"), frustration ("My child isn't even trying"), and stress ("I'm tired of these messes!"). These intense negative emotions can readily combine into a cauldron of smoldering anger. Taking your anger out on your child will feed the very feelings that are making you angry to begin with.

Anger Management Techniques

Use these anger management techniques to calm yourself, and teach some of them to your child, too.

- Take some slow, deep breaths and count to ten.
- Force yourself to smile. The very act of curving your lips into a grin reduces tension.
- Compile a book of jokes and cartoons that strike you as particularly humorous and read them when you are upset.
- Find something funny in the situation.
- Drink a cup of chamomile tea.
- Have a turkey sandwich made with whole wheat bread. The tryptophan and carbohydrate combination induces a sense of well-being.
- Put on some lotion scented with real (not artificial) lavender.
- Play some relaxing music, sit down, close your

eyes, take some slow, deep breaths, and visualize a relaxing scene such as a beach, forest, or expanse of blue sky.

- Put your toddler in a stroller and go for a brisk walk. Exert yourself long enough for your system to release endorphins.

- Pound a pillow, shred old magazines, or club a sturdy tree trunk.

Relaxation Technique

The following quick relaxation technique works wonders for helping parents to feel more centered and grounded when other approaches to meditating fall short. Create an audiotape of instructions by speaking slowly into a recorder. Pause for five seconds between each sentence and insert thirty seconds of silence after each paragraph.

"Close your eyes and notice everything that is touching your skin. Notice the feel of the chair on the back of your legs, the sensations of your feet touching the floor, what your hands are touching. Feel the fabric of your clothes touching your body and of any small sensations of air brushing your face. Try to distinguish the feeling of your hair touching your forehead, ears, or neck.

"Become aware of any sounds that you hear. Listen to any loud noises. Now listen for faint sounds . . . the hum of an appliance, the whoosh of passing cars, the creak of the floor, the rustle of air moving through the room.

"Now concentrate on smells. Try to distinguish any odors in the room. See if you can detect the aroma of food . . . of the carpeting . . . of the air from an open window. Try to detect the scent of your skin, makeup, or perfume.

"Notice any tastes in your mouth. Explore the insides of your cheeks with your tongue. Run your tongue over your teeth and notice the taste of your mouth.

"Open your eyes and look directly ahead. Let your eyes lose focus and relax your eyelids. Without bringing objects into focus or thinking about what you see, try to see the colors, the shades, and the shapes.

"With your eyes still open but unfocused, bring all of the physical sensations you have detected into awareness at once . . . the sensations on your skin . . . the sounds in the room . . . any smells and tastes . . . the colors and shapes before you.

"When you open your eyes, you will feel relaxed and refreshed."

When you feel stressed, play your tape back while sitting in a comfy chair to listen. If you can't manage five minutes alone, see if your toddler will sit down and listen to the tape with you.

Child Power

Although adults are responsible for teaching, coaching, and cheerleading, learning to use the potty really is the child's job. Great teachers cannot make students learn.

Skilled coaches cannot force players to win. The most enthusiastic cheerleaders cannot motivate a team that isn't intent on victory. There is truth to the old saying, "You can lead a horse to water, but you can't make it drink." Adults may be able to force tots to sit on the potty, but they can't make them use it!

Youngsters have minds, hearts, and wills of their own. They encounter different struggles along the way. Everyone learns in time—exactly when that happens, however, is up to each child.

CHAPTER 2
Readiness Skills

If you adopt a very gradual approach and teach about elimination and the potty over time, potty training readiness becomes less of an issue. Your child's emotional resources and maturity are critical factors to consider when you set a date for completing potty training.

Anatomy 101

It's time to bone up on everything you never wanted to know about the bowel and bladder so you can understand what you're up dealing with. Read carefully!

Two donut-shaped muscles called "sphincters" control the flow of waste from the body. The bladder sphincter controls urine, and the anal sphincter controls bowel movements. When the child contracts a sphincter, the donut hole closes up, keeping urine and/or waste inside the body. When he relaxes a sphincter, it opens and waste flows out through the hole.

 FACT

> When the bowel and bladder are overly full, they expel waste automatically. If the pressure on the sphincter muscles becomes too great, they collapse, and the result is an accident.

Normal children eventually learn to control their sphincter muscles, but they can only control them to a certain point. When the bladder or bowel become too full, they expel waste, and the pressure on the sphincters increases until they give way. If a youngster is not on the potty at the moment, she will have an accident.

Toddler boys mature more slowly and finish potty training a few months later than girls, on average. Without any training or help, most children achieve nighttime bowel control first. This happens on its own, as a result of physical maturity. Daytime bowel control usually comes next, perhaps because most youngsters have at least one bowel movement at a predictable time each day so parents can help them get to the bathroom at that time to start teaching them. The contractions of the intestine signaling the start of a bowel movement are often pretty obvious, causing children to grunt and strain, so it is easier for parents and children alike to recognize when a bowel movement is starting.

During bowel movements both sphincters relax, so children urinate and defecate at the same time. By focusing on bowel training, children often become bladder trained at the same time.

A Relaxed Approach

Babies and toddlers do not respond well to pressure, so if you are in a hurry, potty training efforts can backfire and the process can end up taking much longer than if you take a more relaxed approach. To guard against such an unhappy outcome, never try to hurry or pressure a baby. If you have a potty training deadline for your toddler, be sure she is mature enough to follow directions readily, can remain seated for at least five minutes at a stretch, enjoys tasks that make her more independent, persists when learning is hard, and can handle frustration and accidents without losing motivation.

Make sure your child isn't in the midst of dealing with other major issues, such as the arrival of a new baby, the loss of a favorite day care teacher, or a move to a new house. The rule of thumb is to allow at least a month for a youngster to adapt and settle in after a major life change. Since even minor events such as moving from a crib to a regular bed, teething, or having out-of-town guests can throw tots off balance for a few days or weeks, parents should wait until household routines are re-established and their youngster is up to par.

 FACT

> When children have just mastered walking, they are very active. Turmoil intensifies during toddler independence struggles. At both stages, children have a hard time following directions and sitting still. Choose a different time to begin potty training.

Even if all these criteria are met, toddlers are very sensitive to parental anxiety and tension, and react negatively to pressure. You may have to accept that potty training is something you can't rush. When you scale back your expectations, you may well speed learning.

Vocabulary Lessons

Children can begin acquiring the potty training vocabulary they need virtually from birth. Decide what words you plan to use, and be consistent! Even older toddlers become confused when parents use different words for the same thing. When you change diapers, talk to your

infant about what you are doing so he starts to become
familiar with the vocabulary.

Define Your Terms	
Correct Term	**Popular Word**
Toilet	Potty
	Pot
Urine	Pee
	Pee-pee
	Tinkle
	Wee-wee
Urinate	Go pee-pee
Stool, Feces	Poop
	Poo-poo
	Do-do
	Poopy
Defecate, have a	Go poo-poo
bowel movement	Have a B.M.
Penis	Pee-pee
	Thing
	Privates
Vagina	Bottom
	Privates
Buttocks	Bum
	Tush

If you use baby words, don't forget to teach the correct vocabulary when he reaches school age. A third grader may not confess he has a problem because he doesn't know the right term and is too embarrassed to tell you that his "wee-wee" hurts.

Choosing Words

Some parents think it's cute when their toddler refers to waste as "crap" and "piss," but everyone from pediatricians to teachers finds such language offensive. Other parents may not want a youngster who talks that way to associate with their children. Don't use these words at home.

Virtually every toddler goes through the sassy phase of calling people "poopy head" and using other unsavory putdowns. If you respond with shock, anger, or glee, you'll encourage him to repeat them. The idea that particular words and expressions can provoke such a dramatic response from you will intrigue him.

Jan Faull, in her book *Mommy! I Have to Go Potty!* (Raefield-Roberts Publishers, 1996), suggests telling tykes that potty talk belongs in the bathroom. Take your child there, listen patiently as he repeats the forbidden words and phrases, but don't otherwise encourage him. Conclude your little "bull" session by saying you are available to listen whenever he wants to talk, but these words are for use in the bathroom only. After a few sessions, the novelty of saying these words other kids find so funny is supposed to wear off. Hopefully, he'll stop using them around the house, but the parent/child channels of communication remain open. It seems unlikely that toddlers will grasp that it's okay to use certain words in the bathroom but not other places; even preschoolers find coping with two sets of rules very hard. Still, if your child persists in using bathroom words around the house, it may be worth a try.

Ⓔ **QUESTION?**

My child keeps saying naughty words. What can I do?
If ignoring naughty words doesn't stop your child from using them, be firm as you tell him exactly which words you don't like and which are okay. Admonishing him not to talk "like that" is far too general.

If you tell your child that calling people names isn't nice because it hurts their feelings, only very socially sophisticated toddlers will understand. However, even younger ones can understand that it hurts *your* feelings when he calls *you* names. Forbid him to do that. Give him other words to use if he is angry about something, such as, "I'm mad at you, Mom." He must not be allowed to use bathroom words to tease you or anyone else.

Teaching Special Concepts
To teach the difference between wet and dry and between soiled/messy/dirty and clean, use the words

often while washing and drying your child's hands, cleaning up spills, and wiping off spots, as well as when changing diapers. Have your child touch the wet item, as you say "wet" so she can feel it. Get in the habit of asking if her diaper is wet or dry. Show her how to reach inside disposable diapers and feel the crotch. After she answers, check and tell her if she was correct. If she wasn't, give the correct answer and have her check again.

Children also need to know what it means to practice, to relax, to have an accident, and to hurry so they understand what you mean when you say, "Practice sitting on the potty," "Practice relaxing on the potty," "Practice using the potty," "You had an accident," and "Hurry, so you don't have an accident!" They also need to know *how* to hurry, practice, and relax.

Practice makes perfect! To teach that practice is the route to improving, use the word whenever your child is doing something again and again to achieve a goal. For example: "You're practicing eating with a spoon. You're learning to use it"; "You're practicing climbing the stairs. You're getting better at climbing"; "You're practicing putting the puzzle together. You've almost got it!" If your child understands, "Practice sitting on the potty," she'll be less likely to feel punished when told to sit there. Once she understands that the goal is to practice sitting and relaxing, hopefully she won't become frustrated if she doesn't succeed in using the potty instantly.

Just relax! Teach the meaning of relax by saying, "You look relaxed," when your youngster is calm and comfortable so he can associate his feelings and sensations with the word. Teaching him how to relax is harder. When he is upset, suggest he take some deep breaths, sit quietly, and think about something that makes him feel happy. The reason that so many children don't use the potty when their parents have them sit on it and have an accident as soon as they are allowed to get up is because they are too tense to release urine until the session on the potty ends. Having your child sit on the potty is not enough. He must be relaxed in order to be able to release waste.

Hurry up! Most parents use this expression so much, children know all too well what it means. Getting them to hurry to the potty can be tricky. A child constantly pressured to move faster than is comfortable soon learns to resist by throwing on the brakes. Telling her to "Hurry to the potty" may cause her to move more slowly or stop altogether. Try to let your child move at her own pace, and only urge her to hurry when something truly important demands it. This concept is hard for most modern families, but slowing down is good for everybody!

Once children have mastered these concepts, they're well on the way to being potty trained even if they haven't tried sitting on the potty yet. Don't underestimate the importance of teaching the basics!

Giving Directions

When your child knows a basic phrase, such as, "Go to . . ." she will more readily understand a specific direction, such as, "Go to the bathroom." If she is very young, doesn't hear well, or has some other communication difficulty, she must understand gestures and signals so you can communicate with her during potty training.

If your child knows . . .	Your child will understand . . .
"Go to . . . ."	"Go to the potty."
"Tell me when you need/want . . . ."	"Tell me when you need/ want to go to the potty."
"Get some . . . ."	"Get some toilet paper/ clean pants/a sponge/the potty bowl."
"Wipe . . . ."	"Wipe yourself" and "Wipe up the floor."
"Wash . . . ."	"Wash your hands."
"Carry . . . ."	"Carry the potty bowl to the toilet."
"Empty the . . . ."	"Empty the potty bowl."

With a solid foundation for understanding the general direction ("Go to . . . ."), your child will be better able to process the specific direction (" . . . the bathroom.") quickly and accurately. Toddlers are still learning to make sense of one-step directions, such as, "Go to the potty." Two-step directions, such as, "Go to the bathroom and sit down on the potty" may be too much. During potty training, wait until your child completes one step before telling him to do something else.

Improving Compliance

Understanding directions is one thing; following them is quite another. Young toddlers are too busy exploring to sit on the potty. As older toddlers become increasingly intent on pursuing their own interests, they become less reliable about doing what they're told.

It is virtually impossible to potty train a child who won't do what you say. To improve your child's compliance so that she will eventually follow potty training instructions, make an effort to notice when she *does* mind. Comment on each small success and avoid focusing on the times when she isn't doing what she's been told. If you say, "Don't spill your milk!" and she glances at her cup, say, "Good! You're being careful." Later, if the milk gets spilled, give her a sponge so she can help clean it up—and thank her for helping. Similarly, if she's tormenting the cat, show her how to pet it gently. Then praise her for being nice to kitty.

Of all the directions toddlers need to follow during potty training, the hardest is to relax while staying seated on the potty. Fortunately, even hyperactive children stay seated for short stretches, such as in a high chair, car seat, or grocery cart, as well as while watching videos, listening to stories, or playing with toys.

 FACT

If your child is especially contrary and rebellious, learn the fine art of setting and enforcing limits before you attempt potty training. Read *The Everything® Toddler Book* or another book on discipline, or contact your local mental health agency or Head Start program to locate a parenting course.

Make it a policy to ignore your child's restless hands and feet and squirms and wiggles. Reprimands will increase your youngster's nervousness, which will cause him to fidget more, not less. Instead, be positive! Help your child recognize that sitting is something he can do by praising him regularly for staying seated. Point out successes whether they occur in the playroom or the grocery store, and hold small celebrations: "You sat in the grocery cart for five minutes! Congratulations! You're learning! How about a ride on the mechanical pony to celebrate?" Chances are that he'll soon be working to impress you with his ability to sit—assuming he can release energy through physically active play before and after. Be sure he gets plenty of exercise!

Too many parents assume that their child is having trouble remaining seated on the potty due to hyperactivity. The problem usually lies elsewhere. Children are simply full of energy, but don't get enough exercise due to modern lifestyles. Turn off the television, eliminate the caffeine, and make sure your child has lots of time for active play before you ask him to sit on the potty.

Enhancing Sensory Awareness

Children need to be able to sense bladder fullness and recognize when their bowels are starting to move. Around three months of age, some infants can distinguish these sensations, while many toddlers have great difficulty sorting them out. Since disposable diapers mask wetness and obscure the cause-and-effect relationship between elimination and dampness, children may lose touch with their bodies over time. Start potty training your next child when he's a baby or an infant!

Teach your child to recognize the sensations that occur before and during elimination by noticing and commenting when she is relieving herself. If she is always clad in a diaper, noticing can be difficult. Some babies make a face or assume a special posture. Some older toddlers stand with their feet slightly apart and look down. Otherwise, if your child regularly urinates shortly after awakening from a nap or after eating, remove the diaper and see if she will sit on the potty for a bit. If she urinates while sitting on the potty, point out what is happening, and praise her.

It is usually easier to tell when a child is having a bowel movement. Talk her through the whole process to help to increase her awareness of what is happening.

Ⓔ ALERT!

Don't ask your child whether her urine or B.M. is coming out only when you know the answer is yes! Children who don't like their diapers changed may say, "No" and become confused to the point that they don't know the correct answer. Ask at other times, too. Congratulate her for giving the right answer, or correct her gently if she's wrong.

Even if you feel uncomfortable, it is important to describe exactly what is happening:

- "Do you smell that? You're passing gas. You're going to have a B.M."
- "You're grunting. The B.M. is coming. Someday you'll go to the potty when you start grunting."
- "You're putting your B.M. in your diaper."
- "You're all through having a B.M."
- "Your diaper smells. We need to put on a clean one."
- "See? Your B.M. is in your diaper. I'm going to throw it away. Bye-bye, B.M.!"
- "I'm wiping your bottom to clean it. When you're

bigger, you'll clean your bottom with toilet paper."
* "See? This diaper is clean. You smell nice now that your diaper is clean."

Children need to hear these things many times to recognize the sensations preceding bowel movements.

Problem Solving for Tots

Children are bound to have some accidents during potty training. That means trouble if they react by feeling defeated and giving up. Poor self-esteem and difficulties tolerating frustration make this more likely to occur. Help your child develop better persistence by offering a little help and a lot of encouragement whenever he is struggling with any task, such as trying to fit a block into a hole, retrieve a toy that is just out of reach, or get his pants on or off. Provide as little hands-on help as necessary, but encourage him by saying, "Almost . . . you've almost got it . . . hang in there . . . ." At the end, conclude with, "You kept trying and you succeeded!" If he didn't quite make it, provide comfort and reassurance. Tell him to, "Keep practicing! Tomorrow it should be easier."

Little perfectionists may persist well enough, but their lack of patience with themselves and worries about making a mistake can translate into more rather than fewer accidents. Tension and anxiety increase the urinary urge and can prevent them from emptying the bladder completely, so they need to urinate more frequently. Begin teaching the complicated process of handling mistakes in all your child's learning situations, not just those that involve potty training. The steps include seeking help, venting frustration, fixing whatever needs mending, figuring out what went wrong, and figuring out what to do differently next time.

Ⓔ ESSENTIAL

When your child has an accident, help him focus on the lesson, not the mistake. Once he grasps that accidents aren't the end of the world and that no mistake is fatal, it will be easier for him to recover and move on.

Children are born mimics, so a good way to teach the problem-solving steps is to verbalize your thoughts when you make a mistake. "Oops, I dropped the tea cup! Now I have to clean up the broken pieces. It slipped because my hands are wet. Next time I'll dry them before I pick up a cup." "Oops, I pinched your finger in the seatbelt! Can I kiss it to make it better? Next time I'll be sure your hands are out of the way before I buckle you in."

Similarly, when your child has an accident, whether during potty training or at another time, help her understand what went wrong, explain how to repair any damage (having the child participate if possible), and suggest how to avoid the problem in the future. For example, "Uh-oh, your dress is wet. We need to wipe up the floor and change your clothes. You didn't pull up your skirt before you sat on the potty. I need to show you how and help you practice so your dress won't get wet next time."

Encouraging Independence

For children to be motivated to master the potty, they must be able to take pride in achievements that make them more independent. Commend your tot for participating in her own care while you are feeding, dressing, and bathing her. "You put your shirt on by yourself! Such a big girl!" "You are learning to use a spoon instead of your fingers, just like Daddy."

Toddlers go back and forth about wanting to grow up. The truth is that they are still babies. To make growing up less frightening, allow your tot to crumble into your arms when he feels overwhelmed instead of insisting that he act like a big boy. Provide gentle nudges toward independence, but don't push!

Cleanliness

Children lack an inborn aversion to human waste, so the chance to avoid wet and smelly diapers doesn't provide much of a potty training incentive for most of them. Children who wear disposable diapers usually don't feel the wetness. However, if a youngster often removes his diaper or alerts you when he needs to be changed, start potty training him.

Cloth diapers usually enhance youngsters' motivation for potty training because they dislike the sensation of wetness, so it's a good idea to switch from disposable to cloth diapers before potty training. However, some children don't mind wet or soiled cloth diapers either.

Ⓔ ALERT!

Some children dislike diapers because the bulk between their legs inhibits movement. If your youngster persists in removing his diaper for any reason, begin potty training so he can feel comfortable.

Using the potty is far more sanitary than wearing diapers. The bacteria in human waste produce ammonia, which harms the skin and can cause serious rashes. Encourage an appreciation for cleanliness by expressing pleasure over how nice your child looks and smells after a bath or diaper change. Experts advise against doing the reverse, so don't express disgust over dirty diapers and human waste. If a child feels ashamed, he may not want to admit when he needs to use the potty. You definitely need for him to tell you when he needs help to go to the bathroom!

Orderliness

Is your child interested in putting toys and small objects into boxes and cans? Does she enjoy fitting blocks into the correct slots on three-dimensional puzzles? Some people believe that toddlers who like to put one thing inside another, arrange objects, line up toys, and keep things in order are more motivated for potty training.

Certainly if your child fusses when a household object isn't in the "right" place, you can capitalize on his desire for order. Mention when you need to use the toilet and are going to put your urine or B.M. "in the potty where it belongs." When changing soiled diapers, mention that, "Children are supposed to put their B.M.s in the potty," and add that when he gets bigger he'll be able to put his in the potty, too. Have your child watch as you scrape a soiled diaper into the toilet and explain that, "This is where a B.M. belongs." If he is diaperless and begins to relieve himself, see if he can stop while you take him to the potty, so you can help him put it in the "right" place. Not all children can stop urinating once they've started, but some can. Even if your child cannot stop, you can begin implanting the idea that urine is supposed to go in the potty.

Physical Skills

Toddlers need to be able to get their pants up and down quickly. This skill is difficult, and accidents while struggling to remove clothes are common. Have your toddler participate in dressing and undressing as much as possible. Guide her hands to teach the correct motions for raising and lowering pants. Undoing snaps, unzipping zippers, opening Velcro tabs, and maneuvering small buttons out of buttonholes are big challenges for little fingers. Give lots of encouragement when she practices, and don't hurry her.

Social Readiness

Youngsters require a lot of help during the initial phases of potty training, and they must be willing to reach out to others. Teach your child to solicit your assistance. Ask her to call when she needs your help with something, and quickly and attentively respond to her requests.

Ⓔ ESSENTIAL

Wanting to be like Mom or Dad can serve as an important incentive if a youngster can observe them in the bathroom, as can the prospect of sharing progress and victories with important friends and relatives. The desire to copy and impress significant others isn't required for potty training—but it definitely helps!

Both the ability and the desire to imitate others will speed potty training. Many children learn by watching peers, parents, or a doll go through the process. Because younger siblings like to follow older ones around the house and are motivated to do what they do, younger children are usually trained at earlier ages.

Sometimes they manage to learn with very little formal instruction.

Bladder Control

In newborns, the bladder contracts to expel urine when the pressure reaches a certain point. By two to three months of age, they have some bladder control. In 1928, behavioral psychologist James Watson (*Psychological Care of Infant and Child*, W.W. Norton & Company, Inc., 1928) noted that if a small pot was consistently lifted to a newborn baby's bottom when it began urinating, soon it would begin pushing whenever it detected the familiar sensation of the bowl touching its bottom.

Young Babies

Youngsters can achieve daytime continence by age one, according to a 1993 report in the journal *Current Problems in Pediatrics*, although physical capability is only a small part of what is required. Children would have to be worked with consistently from infancy to be continent at such a young age. They would also need to be exceptionally mature. The inability of children this young to delay urination for more than a moment or two translates into accidents, since it is often impossible for them to get to the potty fast enough. Furthermore, young toddlers readily lose control in response to laughing, coughing, sneezing, vigorous exercise, and emotional upset.

Older Babies

Because bladder size increases as children grow, toddlers urinate less often than babies. Once they figure out how to calm bladder contractions and tighten the bladder sphincter simultaneously, they can stave off urination for longer after the urge hits. It takes children a while to discover how full is "too full," so they misjudge how long they can wait before heading to the bathroom.

 FACT

> Learning to use the potty for bowel movements and urination usually happens at the same time. Otherwise, children are likely to learn to have bowel movements in the potty first.

Toddlers can cause themselves to urinate once they figure out how to tense one set of muscles while relaxing another. Telling them to "try" to use the potty won't help, because they won't know how to go about "trying." All parents can do is point out when their child is urinating in an effort to increase his awareness of what is happening.

Parents can estimate bladder functioning by watching for certain signs.

- **Your child's diapers remain dry for one to two hours at a stretch during the day**. More frequent urination makes training more difficult. If your child leaks urine, it may be caused by a physical abnormality, but more often its cause is a bladder infection. See your doctor immediately.

- **Your child urinates large quantities at one time**. This signals that the sphincter is able to contain urine properly. If the stream is not strong and steady when your child urinates a lot, notify your doctor.

- **Your child can stop the flow of urine midstream**. Not all toddlers can, but having mastered this tricky maneuver means they can tense and relax the bladder sphincter at will. That can reduce the number of accidents—assuming they can remember how to stop when the urge to urinate is strong. Most children panic.

- **Your child awakens in response to a full bladder**. This awakening means the sensations of bladder fullness are strong enough to rouse the sleeping brain. Children who cannot wake up have problems with bedwetting.

- **Your child awakens dry after naps and/or in the morning**. This symptom suggests that bladder size is normal and that urine production decreased during sleep, as it should. If hormone levels are insufficient to suppress urine production, children must make many trips to the bathroom during the night or wet the bed.

- **It is obvious when your child is about to urinate or defecate**. It's not always obvious, but if it is, parents can try to help youngsters get to the potty on time.

Although children can make a lot of progress with bladder control during the first year or two of life if they are consistently worked with, an occasional daytime accident is to be expected until age three. Bedwetting can remain a problem if the sensation of a full bladder isn't strong enough to rouse a sleeping brain. Even at age five, approximately 15 to 20 percent of youngsters continue to wet the bed.

Bowel Control

Contractions reflexively expel the contents of a newborn's bowel (the meconium) during the first day or two of life. Soon after, many infants can be observed pushing to help a bowel movement along. They have three to nine movements per day, depending on how often they eat. Breast milk usually causes looser stool than formula.

Toddlers can push willfully, but may not know how to relax the sphincter muscle to release stool. As with controlling the bladder, learning how to tense some muscles while relaxing others can be hard for children to master.

Two signs of physical readiness will make bowel training much easier. First, your child's stool should be well formed. Children won't have enough warning to get to the bathroom on time if they have diarrhea or very loose stool. It is important that children not be constipated during potty training because hard stool can be painful. Extreme constipation can cause uncontrollable leakage as watery stool seeps around the hard mass and out the rectum. See your doctor if your child has this condition. Second, your child should be able to communicate that a bowel movement is starting. If children are aware of bowel movement sensations, bowel training is easier.

ⓔ QUESTION?

How often do children have bowel movements?
Patterns differ dramatically from one infant to the next. Some have many B.M.s each day; some average less than one a day. The consistency of the stool is more important than the frequency. Stool that is too hard or too loose complicates potty training.

Parent Readiness

Potty training will be easier and faster if you decide in advance what your child needs to learn and how you will teach it. No matter what method you use, the keys are kindness and consistency. To help ensure you remain kind, choose a time when you feel emotionally centered and can be patient. Otherwise, your child will react to your tension and have difficulty concentrating. To provide consistency, all caregivers need to participate, use the same approach, and work on potty training regularly. When training is sporadic, children become confused as to what is expected of them, and the habit of using the potty each and every time takes much longer to develop.

Daring to Differ

Perhaps Mom wants "her" child to experience the later, softer, gentler approach to potty training while Dad thinks that kind of coddling will ruin him for life. Or Mom is sick to death of laundry and wants to get this potty training show on the road and Dad is saying she'll break his spirit and turn him into a chronic people-pleaser by pushing too hard. How can a couple reconcile two such very different philosophies?

 ALERT!

Arguing with your spouse about which potty training method to use will hurt your child more than using a method that is either stricter or less strict than she really needs. Read this book in its entirety and try for one last meeting of the minds, then seek couple's counseling to reconcile your differences if necessary.

The potty-practice method (Chapter 5) may be a program you can agree upon. Your child spends time relaxing in the bathroom for three to five minutes every hour or two, but can avoid that requirement if he goes to the potty on his own beforehand, and he can leave sooner if he uses the potty and washes his hands before his time is up. If that method isn't agreeable to both of you, consider letting the indulgent parent handle the laundry and use the potties-without-pressure method (Chapter 7) for six months, then have the stricter parent give the potty practice or fast-track method a whirl (Chapter 6). Agree to support one another no matter which one of you is in charge at the moment. You need to respect what each of your child-rearing approaches has to offer. Battling for control of your child's bowel and bladder accomplishes nothing.

In-home Helper

Discussing intimate bodily functions makes some parents feel as if they're breaking a taboo. Their desire not to discuss this delicate subject can create real problems if children have worries, anxieties, or concerns about having bowel movements in the potty—and many do.

One way to make discussions easier is to begin by reading the children's storybook *Everybody Poops* to your child. The book can still be a shocker to adults due to the straightforward explanations (e.g., "An elephant makes a big poop. A mouse makes a tiny poop."). They may find the cartoon pictures of animal poop and the contents of a soiled diaper too graphic for their taste, too, yet children find the book engaging. Sharing this book with your child can prepare you for the kind of frank discussions about potties and elimination you will need to have. It has served as a miracle cure for many nervous toddlers because it answers their unspoken questions and relieves their anxieties. It can be particularly effective in helping them overcome feelings of shame, a most difficult emotion that is a major force behind some children's staunch refusal to have bowel movements in the potty.

Multiple Caregivers

As stated before, the two basic rules of potty training are kindness and consistency. Consistency can be especially hard to come by if your child spends a lot of time with other caregivers, and this situation is undoubtedly part of the reason that so many modern children are trained so late. Until children develop the habit of using the potty, a caregiver must be responsible for prompting them. Otherwise, youngsters have to remain conscious of their bladder at every moment, and that takes more energy and a better ability to concentrate than most little folks have.

It is best for all your child's caregivers to use the same program. What is desirable isn't always possible, but there are several things you can do to increase the likelihood that other adults will follow your program. Write out exactly what you're doing at home or buy more copies of this book, bookmark the chapters, and underline the relevant passages that day care center teachers, baby sitters, and the "other parent" need to know. Set aside some uninterrupted time with other caregivers to discuss potty training so you're both on the same page.

Make it easy for others to cooperate by supplying everything they need to be able to follow your rules. For instance, for the potty-practice method, provide an alarm clock they can set so they don't forget to put your child on the potty at certain times; give them a list of times, too. Provide a timer they can use to signal when your child can get off the potty a few minutes later, a calendar for keeping track of successes and accidents, a stock of rewards, a sticker chart, and extra changes of clothes in case of accidents.

Ⓔ ESSENTIAL

Some children will use their potty at home but refuse to use strange ones. In that case, a portable potty may help. If your child can become accustomed to using it at home, he may be willing to use it other places, too.

A contentious ex-spouse may insist on doing things differently, but follow your program without telling you. If you cannot work together, see Mom's Method in Chapter 8 for suggestions about how to handle an older toddler to get him to follow the rules in your house when he can do as he pleases elsewhere.

Hygiene Training

Potty training is more than just eliminating into a potty. In a broader sense, it is about maintaining cleanliness in order to prevent illness and safeguard health, as well as maintaining basic standards of personal hygiene so as not to offend others. Parents and caregivers need to teach youngsters the procedures to follow for wiping, flushing, potty-bowl rinsing, and hand washing (Chapter 9). Remember that good personal hygiene is the result of consistent training.

The Big Step Forward

Wanting something and being ready for it are two different things. Many parents who want their child to be trained by a particular age or before a special deadline soon discover they don't have the time and energy required to make their goal realistic.

Even if you do have the time and energy, they are only part of what you need to potty train your child. What you also need is to proceed with kindness, patience, consistency, and an upbeat, positive attitude!

Chapter 3
All the Right Stuff

Special potty training story-books, videos, dolls, under-pants, chairs, and stepping stools thrill toddlers and help motivate them to leave diapers behind and join the world of big people. Whenever possible, let them help choose the kinds they like.

Buying a Potty

Although a number of commercial products can make life easier, the only must-have item for potty training is a potty. In days gone by, a simple pot or bowl sufficed for everyone, but the added comfort and appealing colors of commercial brands enhance toddlers' motivation. Shopping at garage sales and discount stores can be a good way to save money.

 ALERT!

> If you start training early, a simple pot works for babies and small toddlers. Find one that is short enough so that your child's feet rest comfortably on the ground, narrow enough at the top so he doesn't fall in, and with a wide base so it doesn't tip over. The top rim should be wide, too, so as not to cut off circulation in the legs.

Two basic types of commercial potties are available. *Potty chairs* are self-contained units that sit on the floor. They are low enough to increase children's feelings of security, and increase a toddler's interest by being for her exclusive use. The disadvantage is that a removable bowl must be carried to the toilet, emptied, and rinsed after each use. Also, some children struggle with the transition from the potty chair to the regular toilet. *Potty seats* attach to the seat of a regular toilet, creating a smaller opening so children don't fall in. Some toddlers like the feeling of being grown up that comes from using the toilet like older siblings and parents, but some youngsters are afraid of the height. Climbing up can be difficult, and a scary fall can complicate training.

Take your youngster with you when you buy a potty so you can check the fit and hopefully choose one he likes. Here are some features to look for:

❏ **Stability**—The base of a potty chair should be at least as wide as the top for toddlers, and wider at the base than the top for babies. Have your youngster lean in all directions while sitting on it to make sure that the chair stays firmly on the floor.

❏ **Splash guards**—Although splash guards are a boon for sanitation by directing the stream of urine, which is especially useful for boys, many tots end up with a painful bump at some point, and won't want to go near the potty afterward. Climbing over a splash guard to get off the potty seat can be tricky enough to cause a fall. Splash guards should be padded or detachable. Otherwise, make sure there is an inch between the splash guard and the child's crotch.

❏ **Security**—Potty seats should fasten to the toilet seat securely. Check the grips.

❏ **Potty bowl**—Bigger is better for preventing spills. The bowl should be easy enough to remove so that toddlers can empty them on their own.

❏ **Seat**—A cold, hard seat is less inviting than a soft one. Look for a model with a cushioned seat.

❑ **Arm rests**—If potty chairs have arm rests, children will automatically reach for one and lean on it as they sit down, which can cause the chair to overturn. Avoid them.

❑ **Stepping stool**—Some potty chairs convert to stepping stools, which children can use when they begin using the toilet. Some potty seats have attached stepping stools for ease in climbing up onto the toilet.

❑ **Transition options**—Some potty chairs convert to potty seats, which can save money down the road.

❑ **Musical potties**—Some potties play a song when wet, so parents know when urination has occurred. However, babies twist around to see where the music is coming from, which creates a mess and increases the chance that they may fall off. They may work for toddlers, however.

❑ **Portability**—Some potty chairs and seats fold down for traveling. Be sure that the hinges are sturdy so the unit won't collapse during normal use.

Some children totally reject one potty, refusing even to go near it, yet are very taken with another brand. Ask about the return policy and save your receipt!

Potty Training Aids

Again, the training method you use, the age and temperament of your child, and your own comfort with coaching your child through the training process will determine what items you will need. Although they are not essential, the following potty training aids will make the teaching easier:

- **Baby doll**—A doll that wets and comes with its own underpants and baby bottle is ideal for demonstrating the process of using the potty.
- **Baby wipes**—When wiping themselves after a bowel movement, children do a better job with moistened towelettes than toilet paper.
- **Books**—Storybooks about potties can increase children's interest, teach the process, and help them to resolve their tangled emotions about giving up diapers.

To help your child's motivation as well as your own, do what you can to make the learning experience as fun and easy as possible.

Training Attire

It might not seem obvious at first, but your child's ability to undress and dress herself plays a large role in her training progress. A good potty training wardrobe consists of clothes toddlers can remove easily and quickly.

Pull-Ups

Most parents automatically buy disposable pull-ups, or training pants as they are sometimes called, but these aren't usually a good idea. Disposables are so absorbent, youngsters have a hard time feeling the wetness, which slows learning. Disposables also keep them from experiencing the cold, damp discomfort of wet cloth, which can motivate them to stay dry. While disposables are more likely to thwart potty training than help it along, they can be useful as night wear for children who resist being put in diapers but continue to wet the bed.

Ⓔ ESSENTIAL

Toddlers are very motivated by the opportunity to wear regular underpants. Let your child choose the kind she likes. Action figures and cartoon characters are popular.

Cloth pull-ups or training pants have more padding in the crotch than regular underwear. If leakage is a problem, add a waterproof diaper cover.

PODS

The problem with going straight from diapers to underwear is that there are bound to be some accidents. Potty on Discreet Strips, PODS, reduce the mess from accidents.

PODS adhere to your child's underpants using an adhesive strip, like that on a sanitary napkin. Although they are absorbent enough to contain the trickles and puddles, they allow children to feel the wetness from the accident. PODS also allow air circulation through the underpants so the pads quickly cool—that's a much better deterrent to accidents than the warm, cozy feeling of wet diapers. PODS are available from ✍ *www.pottytrainingsolutions.com.*

Clothes

Pants with elastic waistbands and Velcro closures are easiest for tots to get on and off. Zippers and snaps are harder; buttons are hardest. Learning to pull tight pants over a round bottom is a challenge, so provide oversized jeans, warm-up pants, slacks, and rompers. Skirts are ideal for girls.

Ⓔ **ESSENTIAL**

> Long tops get wet during accidents. Although they can be rolled up and pinned to help keep them dry during training, short tops are ideal.

Make sure your child has lots of chances to practice getting clothes on and off. If you usually let him help when you dress and undress him, he'll get good practice, and going to the potty will be much easier. Although you may be in a hurry for him to get his clothes on and off, try not to rush him so that he can concentrate on developing the fine motor coordination he needs.

Rewards

When your smiles and applause begin to lose their charm, a little treat can sometimes spark motivation. Regardless of which treat or reward you choose, be sure to stock up in advance!

- Stickers to affix to a wall chart, calendar, or even to the potty itself. Print out a free chart from ✑*www.ablebaby.com* or photocopy one from Appendix B.
- A coin to drop in the piggy bank or home gumball machine.
- A chance to select a wrapped gift from a basket grab-bag style.
- A small toy. Hot Wheels are a favorite.
- An M&M or small candy. Though motivating kids with junk food really is not a good idea, for some youngsters a sweet treat is the only reward that really works.

Children are often ambivalent about the potty because they lose the special, undivided attention they used to get during diaper changes. To make up for the loss of these precious moments and to reward potty successes, read a book, play a game of pat-a-cake, or sing "Itsy-Bitsy Spider" afterward.

Bathroom Safety

Once formal potty training begins, youngsters will be spending a lot of time in the bathroom. Place a teetering toddler high on a potty seat in a cramped space with slippery floors and hard porcelain, and her risk of getting hurt in a fall increases dramatically. Careful baby proofing is a must.

- Outfit floors with skid-proof flooring and mats.
- Place a carpet around the potty to cushion falls.
- Place rubberized decals on the side of the tub and toilet.
- Clear a path from your child's bedroom to the toilet.
- Put a safety clip on the toilet seat to deter toddlers from playing in the toilet.

Babies and young toddlers must be supervised in the bathroom at all times. Even with careful baby proofing, the bathroom may be too dangerous for wobbly walkers to handle alone, especially if they like to climb. Consider moving the potty chair to another room of the house.

Water Safety
Babies and toddlers can drown by falling into toilet bowls—even children who can swim will panic. With their face in the water they can't make a sound, so parents may not discover the mishap until it's too late. Do not let your child use the toilet unsupervised!

Toddlers find the toilet bowl irresistible. Their splashing makes the floor slippery, which increases the danger of falling down or in. Teach other family members to keep the door closed at all times. If you use a potty seat, you must remain present to make sure your baby doesn't try to stand on it, or decide to play in her waste, which babies find fascinating.

ESSENTIAL

Hold your child tightly when she uses a toilet without a potty seat. Besides the risk of drowning, a tumble into cold water can cause an enduring phobia. If you cannot afford a specially designed potty chair or seat, place a small pot or bowl on the floor for your child to sit on.

Night Safety

Use night lights to illuminate the bedroom, hall, and bathroom to ease the way for your nighttime traveler. Glow-in-the-dark adhesive strips or a potty light not only light the path, but also may be novel enough to draw your child toward the target.

All You Really Need

The two things you really need most right now—a ready and willing child and a positive mental attitude—cannot be bought in a store. Unfortunately, there's not much that can be done about the former. Some youngsters delight in new experiences and eagerly embrace change, while others cling to tried-and-true habits and routines, and are very reluctant to let them go. What you can do something about is your attitude. Fortunately, that is not as difficult as it might seem.

Since your child will in fact be potty trained, the question really is not whether or not you will achieve your final goal, but how. The following chapters describe very different methods. Whichever you choose, promise yourself that come what may, you will remain committed to enjoying the time you spend with your child. If you keep that promise, you will have the most valuable potty training aid of all.

Chapter 4
Baby-Track Method

It's back to the future with the baby-track method. These age-old techniques operate under the premise that early exposure and consistent practice help children master important new skills, from talking to eating with a spoon. Potty training really isn't that different.

Early Learning Benefits

Experts advise parents to talk, sing songs, and recite nursery rhymes to boost language skills, even though very young babies do not understand what they hear. Similarly, babies are supposed to help feed themselves so they can learn how to eat without help, never mind that they wave the spoon like a flag with one hand while tossing food with the other. Yet when it comes to potty training, most experts suggest not doing anything before age two. If this same logic were applied to eating, no youngster would be allowed to hold a spoon until around age four, when most have enough control to learn quickly. Start potty training early to speed learning during the toddler years. You could even end up with a potty-trained baby!

Most parents are capable of providing the kinds of relaxed, fun early learning experiences that instill healthy attitudes toward elimination and the potty, teach important concepts, and provide practice with potty skills. Many babies actually begin using the potty or another receptacle regularly after they've been on the baby track for a short time, and there is nothing to suggest that they are hurt by such an early introduction.

As recently as the 1920s, parents in the United States began potty training their infants at three to ten months of age by holding their infant over a sink, basin, toilet, potty, or other receptacle, making sure to provide adequate and comfortable support.

A Compassionate Approach

The accepted age for potty training has increased over the last century. Claudine Brown, mother of two, worked with dozens of children at an orphanage in the 1930s. She reports that the accepted practice was for parents to begin accustoming children to the potty soon after they learned to walk, so they were "basically" trained a few months later—meaning that they still needed help with clothing, and an occasional accident was to be expected.

Ⓔ ALERT!

Toilet training accidents have been cited as the leading catalyst of serious abuse of children over age one, according to a 1994 article in *Your Health* entitled, "The Potty Wars." When working with a baby or young toddler, keep your cool!

Many parents today assume the techniques must have been harsh or punitive, but this was not the case. If mistreated, children didn't learn very well, and their emotional upsets often meant they continued to have accidents and problems with the potty at age three or four. The workable method was for parents to try to get their baby to the potty at the right time and have them sit there for a few minutes. If nothing happened, the children would play for a bit before trying again.

The period from birth to age three is a critical time

for psychological development. The self-concept and feelings of self-worth children acquire during these few short years can continue into adulthood. If caregivers react with even mild frustration, disappointment, or irritation, babies detect their negative emotions. Given the intimate nature of elimination, parents' impatience and anger during potty training can have harmful, far-reaching consequences. When working with a baby, you must be supportive and gentle!

"The keys to working with little ones," Brown says, "are time, persistence, patience, and lots of love and understanding." Back then, most children were potty trained by the time they could walk. Since one of Brown's nephews learned to walk at a very young age, he was potty trained at eight months.

Sphincter Control

Most parents believe that sphincter control does not develop until late in the toddler years, so they think babies cannot accomplish much. Traditional practices prove them wrong, as does the fact that throughout most of the modern world, infants eliminate into little pots and are usually trained well before age two. Babies urinate frequently but do not leak, as some pediatric experts in the United States have suggested. As the bladder grows, it holds more liquid and potty training is easier when urination is less frequent. Toddlers are so difficult to work with, however, baby training remains the method of choice in other countries and is again gaining popularity in the United States.

Assorted Skills for Babies

Even if babies are too young or small to have the physical ability or attention span to sit on the potty, parents can do other things to help them learn basic skills they need to be potty trained.

- When you go the toilet, place your baby on a blanket on the floor near you, and explain what you are doing: pulling down underpants, sitting down, urinating or moving your bowels, getting toilet paper, wiping yourself clean, flushing, and washing. With many repetitions, babies will understand the vocabulary and process.

- Talk your baby through diaper changes, being careful to keep the vocabulary consistent. "Let's see if your diaper is wet. Is it wet? I'm feeling your diaper. Yes! It's wet." "Let's see if your diaper has B.M. in it. Does it? Yes, I smell the B.M.! Mommy needs to change it. She's taking off your diaper. See the B.M.? (Hold up the diaper.) This is baby's B.M. Yes it is!"

- When teaching the names for parts of the body (e.g., "Where is Baby's tummy?" There it is!"), add the genitals. For example, "Where is Baby's penis? There it is!" "Where is Baby's bottom? There it is!"

- When teaching the function of body parts (e.g., "How does Baby see? With his eyes!" "How does Baby hear? With his ears!"), add, "How does Baby make pee-pee? With his penis."

- Conclude each diaper change by cleaning your

baby's hands with water or a baby wipe so she starts forming the habit of washing after she uses the potty.

If your baby commonly begins wetting or releasing stool when diapers are off, keep a small pot or bowl near the changing table and bath. Pick him up and hold him over it, and happily explain what is happening: "Daddy's baby is urinating in the pot! Yes! What a champ!" Again, your actions and tone matter more than your words. If the timing is right so that your baby urinates in his pot many times, and if your smiles and praise let him know that you are pleased, he may figure out what is happening. If you bring him the potty bowl when he has been dry for a while and has urine in his bladder, he may begin pushing to make himself urinate in it.

The Happiest Students

An ideal time to begin potty training is after babies can sit up by themselves but before they can walk. Once tykes start toddling about on their own, they are constantly on the move, and it is harder to get them to sit still and relax on the potty. If they're already accustomed to the potty when they begin walking, they may be delighted to use their two newly-mobile legs to take themselves there.

Introducing the Potty

While carrying your baby to the potty, speak excitedly to communicate that you have a wonderful surprise for her: "You're going to sit on your potty! Isn't that wonderful?" Your tone matters far more than the words, of course. Your exclamations of delight on seeing your little darling sitting there will probably be enough to convince her that she is doing something wonderful. If so, you will probably see a broad smile and excited waving of arms and legs.

A Captive Audience

After babies have learned to sit up by themselves and before they learn to walk, two things are certain. Youngsters like to socialize, and their social calendars tend to be pretty empty! One thing they do enjoy is impressing the big people in their lives. Sitting on the potty can give them that chance. Babies do not exactly have lots of activities on their agenda, and are usually far more agreeable than toddlers to staying put for a few minutes.

Ⓔ ESSENTIAL

> For the baby-track method, children must be able to sit on their own without slouching, listing, tilting, or needing a prop for at least thirty minutes. Until your baby can sit by herself, she is not ready to sit on the potty!

Potty Fear

If your baby is reluctant to try new things, place the potty in the play area for a few days so he can see it.

Put a stuffed animal in the bowl and say, "Peek-a-boo!" as you lift it out. After a few days of assorted games, try sitting him on it. The sensation of cold plastic on a bare bottom can be very disconcerting, so leave the diaper on the first few times you put your baby on the potty. Since potty chairs are low to the floor and hot air rises, they are usually much cooler than parents anticipate. If his potty is small enough, it may be possible to sit him on it and hold him on your lap while reading him a story. If he wants to get off, remove him from the potty before he cries or gets upset. One bad experience can take a long time to overcome.

Ⓔ ESSENTIAL

If you get a little smile when you put your high-strung baby on the potty, smile back and remove her quickly. Make sure all of her experiences are positive so she will gladly sit there again.

Potty Fun

Babies love to impress their parents. They love being cute. They adore showing off. If you let your baby know just how cute she is as she sits on her little potty, however briefly, she will soon decide it is a great place to sit. If you play pat-a-cake or "So Big," or initiate a Mommy's-gonna-tickle-you game, her staying power may well rival yours.

Ⓔ FACT

Using the potty is far more hygienic for babies than wearing diapers. In fact, using the potty is the best cure for diaper rash. Also, the toxins that leach from disposable diapers and the harsh chemicals used to clean cloth diapers can cause allergic reactions.

Babies can have fun engaging in the games parents invent to make sitting on the potty enjoyable, or they can feel overwhelmed and discouraged when they are expected to fulfill demands they cannot even fathom. Your baby's self-esteem depends on your ability to create reasonable goals.

- Keep the tone of every learning session relaxed.
- Quit the minute your baby loses interest.
- Do not insist that your baby sit on the potty when she wants off.

Place a blanket or carpet under the potty to prevent a hard bump from a fall. Above all else, end each session *before* your baby fusses.

On the Potty

Gradually trade the games and antics for relaxed conversation. Then provide a small toy so your baby can spend a few moments entertaining himself. The long-range goal is for your child to sit quietly for ten or fifteen minutes. It can take a week or several months to get to this point. Even then, never leave him unattended. If he falls, you may be back to square one. If he resists sitting on the potty for whatever reason, give him a break for a week or two before trying again.

Establishing Patterns

Place your baby on the potty when you expect him to urinate or have a bowel movement. Many youngsters eliminate like clockwork soon after awakening or about twenty minutes after a meal. If you don't know his patterns, remove the diaper for a day so you can see when he relieves himself and record the times. Be forewarned: This is likely to be a very messy day. Then, make an effort to put him on his little potty at times he is most likely to need to use it.

Regulating Patterns

If your baby sips and snacks all day long, his patterns may be too erratic to predict when he might need to use the potty. In that case, put him on the potty after his first morning meal and after naps. You may also want to talk to your pediatrician about whether eliminating snacking might be better for your baby's overall health. Even so, some children's systems are just naturally irregular.

Remember that although it's great if your baby actually uses the potty when you set him on it, the goal is just to help him get comfortable sitting there. Consider how hard it is to get many toddlers over their fear of the potty, and you'll realize how much your baby has accomplished.

First Successes

If you regularly place your youngster on the potty when you expect her to urinate or have a bowel movement, and she sits for ten minutes, one or the other (if not both!) of the desired results will occur. Given the difficulty many parents have getting toddlers to sit still long enough for such a coincidence to occur, these happy accidents are important!

Ⓔ **ESSENTIAL**

If you really ham it up and praise your baby when he voids or has a bowel movement in the potty, you will encourage him to respond in a similar fashion the next time you put him on the potty. Some babies respond more enthusiastically to silliness than praise.

When your baby uses the potty and you react with enthusiasm, she won't understand what she did that created such excitement and pleased you so. It's like smiling—babies smile accidentally and don't realize they have done something special until you respond with

delight. After a few more accidental smiles and enthusiastic responses from parents, babies begin to associate
their action (smiling) with their parents' reaction.
Eventually they smile on purpose in hopes of getting
others to smile and coo at them.

Ⓔ QUESTION?

**Will early potty training make a parent's
life easier?**
In an age of disposable diapers, a potty-
trained baby may not reduce your workload.
You will have to keep track of when she might
need to use the potty, get her there in time,
undress and dress her, and clean her up.

After your baby makes the association between using
the potty and your enthusiastic response, he will automatically push to try to empty his bowel and bladder
when you put him on the potty in hopes that you will
respond with approval, delight, or by doing something he
enjoys, such as being tickled. If anything is in his bowel
or bladder, it will come out when he pushes. When you
know his patterns and get him onto the potty before
urine and stool accumulate to the point that his body
automatically expels waste, you can avoid accidents.

How often you can put your baby on the potty will
depend on your family schedule. If you work, put him
on the potty for a few minutes each morning for a once-
a-day practice, or add a second practice after dinner.

How soon using the potty becomes a habit depends on how often he is placed there and uses it. Putting a baby who is ill on the potty is a bad idea, unless he insists or has trouble bringing himself to go in a diaper.

Ordinarily, it will not make sense to put a tired, cranky baby on the potty, unless he wants to use it. Your baby's overall health, well-being, and desire to participate should always be the primary considerations.

Potty Signals

When babies develop a conditioned response to the potty, they automatically begin to push as soon as their bottoms touch the potty. They do not decide to push. The response is involuntary. If your baby is not pushing automatically, it's probably because she's not using it regularly enough, but who cares? The point is to help her develop a positive attitude toward potties and elimination, become aware of bodily functions, and practice sitting on the potty.

Ⓔ ESSENTIAL

Even if you put your baby on the potty only once or twice per day, your baby can learn the purpose of the potty, practice using it, and can come to accept the potty as part of the daily routine. That can make training easier during the toddler years.

Once babies understand the purpose of the potty, they may begin to signal when they need it. Your child may wriggle, flush, or make a special cry. After a while, your baby may turn toward the potty, reach for it, wave, or look at it and fuss, just as he does when he wants a bottle or toy. Watch for a signal and respond immediately.

Teaching Signals

Teach your baby to signal when she needs the potty by encouraging her to reach for it before you put her on it. Hold her hands in yours so you reach for it together. In time she will reach for it when she wants to use it, just as she reaches for her bottle when she is hungry.

Cueing Your Baby

Help your baby learn to use the potty on cue by making a special sound such as "ssss" or "shshsh" every time she is relieving herself, even if she is wetting her diaper or having an accident. She will come to associate the sound you make with elimination. Eventually you will get to the point that when you put her on the potty and make the special sound, she will push to try to go. If she is able to use the potty, praise her heartily! She can't use it unless she has waste in her system, so don't be upset if nothing happens. Don't be upset if she has an accident shortly after you take her off the potty, either. Learning takes time.

If a baby acts as if she wants the potty but does

not use it, perhaps she wanted to play with it. It's good for her to like her potty, so sanitize it and let her play!

Ⓔ ESSENTIAL

> After a month or two of you helping a baby reach for the potty, she should start looking toward it or reaching for it when she wants it. Respond quickly, and praise her lots if she ends up using it.

Missed Signals

When your baby signals for the potty, his need to urinate or have a bowel movement may be imminent, so you must get him to it fast. However, babies often misinterpret their physical sensations. Just as they fail to signal when they need to use the potty, or do not signal in time, they sometimes signal when they don't need it at all. And sometimes, babies just need a few minutes so they can relax enough to use it.

Even young toddlers who have figured out which muscles to use to "hold it" for a minute or two will not always remember how. If they try to crawl or walk to the potty by themselves, they may get distracted en route. Even if they go directly to the potty the moment the urge hits, they won't always make it in time. Babies are even less predictable. Expect accidents!

Before potty training, your baby may have slept through the night without a problem. After he starts using the potty, he may awaken and cry during the night because he needs to use it. Anytime a baby who has been using the potty becomes cranky, put him on the potty before trying other ways to calm him.

 ALERT!

> If your baby's stool is looser than normal or he has diarrhea, he may need to wear diapers for a time. Strings of accidents during stressful periods are to be expected. Sometimes babies simply stage a "potty strike," and parents never do figure out why they suddenly refuse to use it.

Oops!

Just as Fido begins salivating the minute his master reaches for the bag of dog food and Fluffy appears in the kitchen and meows every time her mistress opens a can of anything, a baby may begin urinating or having a bowel movement the moment her diaper is removed instead of waiting to be placed on the potty. Don't scare her as you dive for cover. Avoid any sort of harsh or rough handling, angry words, shouts, or reprimands. Make your special sound, such as "ssss" or "shshsh" whenever and wherever she is relieving herself so she associates her act with your sound. In the future, wait to remove the diaper until you have carried her to the potty. Add smiles and nods and coos of delight when she uses it. Otherwise, just make the special sound while she relieves herself and clean her up without comment. In time she will be conditioned to wait for the potty.

Potty Strikes

Perhaps a baby who has really been enjoying the potty suddenly fusses the minute he is placed on it and wants to get off. Perhaps last time he fell off and bumped his head or a sibling burst into the room and startled him. Perhaps he's getting sick. Perhaps he just doesn't feel like it. It doesn't matter why a baby does not want to sit on the potty—it only matters that he doesn't. Remove him!

Ⓔ **QUESTION?**

What if my baby goes on a potty strike that lasts for days?
Stop putting him on the potty for a week before trying again. If he still resists, wait a month before reintroducing the potty gradually. Even if he goes many months without using it, you will see during the toddler years that he benefited from his early training.

If your baby is busy playing and refuses to go to the potty, tell him you must put on a diaper so he doesn't make a mess, and change him immediately. Do not be mad if he fusses and cries, but don't let him continue playing until he's been changed. Let him choose whether he will use the potty right now or put on a diaper right now.

When your baby learns to walk, encourage your young toddler to use the potty by letting him participate more in the tasks he enjoys, such as getting toilet paper, wiping himself, emptying the potty bowl, and flushing. Help him with the chores he dislikes, such as dressing and washing his hands.

 ALERT!

> Babies often have potty training setbacks once they start walking. They are too excited about exploring to take time out to go to the potty. Be patient!

Growing Up

Once your baby uses the potty most of the time, she can wear training pants instead of diapers. When she signals that she wants her potty after she has learned to crawl, put it two feet away and call her to it so she can begin learning to crawl toward it when she needs it. That way, when she is walking, she'll know to take herself, though she will still need help with dressing and cleanup. Do not be surprised if you feel you are a slave to your young toddler's bowel and bladder. You'll still have to help your child remove her clothes, wipe herself, put her clothes back on, empty the potty bowl into the toilet, flush, and wash her hands until she's old enough to handle everything herself. Your job as a parent is far from done!

Chapter 5

Potty-Practice Method

For this method, you gently but matter-of-factly intro- duce your child to the potty and teach each step of the process. To be successful, this method requires getting your child to the potty at times he needs to use it and teaching him to sit still and relax enough so that he actu- ally can go.

An Overview

For the potty-practice method, parents teach toddlers age eighteen months or older the readiness skills in Chapter 2. They provide a very gradual introduction to the potty, present basic lessons about bowel movements and urination, and hold regular potty practice sessions. During potty practice sessions tots sit on the potty at scheduled times, relax, and handle assorted chores, such as undressing, wiping, dressing, removing the potty bowl, emptying it into the toilet, flushing, replacing the potty bowl, washing hands, etc. Because potty practice sessions can be held to fit busy schedules, this method is workable for most families. Most of the time is spent on the area toddlers find most challenging: sitting still and relaxing.

Scheduled Practices Are Important

Modern families often exist in a state of chaos with no fixed time for anything, but toddlers do better with routines. Holding regularly scheduled potty practices can seem too taxing, but they can help regulate your child's system. It is worth the effort to ensure that your child eats, sleeps, exercises, and uses the potty at the same times every day. You could end up with not only a potty-trained child, but a calmer, happier family.

Stay Flexible

If your child catches on quickly and is highly self-motivated, there is no need to plod on through the program and continue to hold lots of potty practices. Consider switching to the potties-without-pressure method described in Chapter 7. On the other hand, to speed things up you might try some techniques from the fast-track toddler method described in Chapter 7. Stay flexible!

 FACT

> Most toddlers urinate shortly after awakening and about twenty minutes after eating. Otherwise, they urinate about once every two hours. You need to determine when your child usually has bowel movements and urinates. Hold a potty practice when you expect your child to have a B.M. Hold additional practices at as many other times when you expect him to urinate as you possibly can.

What to Expect

If an eighteen-month-old finishes training fast, he will continue to need help with clothing for quite some time, and may continue to have an occasional accident when his timing is off or he struggles with clothing. You must continue to supervise unless your bathroom has been thoroughly baby-proofed. Good baby-proofing will probably mean your child must use a potty chair instead of a potty seat so that the regular toilet can remain locked.

How Long?

How long a toddler will need in order to finish training depends on a number of factors, especially the frequency of the practice sessions and the child's maturity level, temperament, and motivation. Frequent practices can speed learning if the child is cooperative. Working parents might start on a weekend so they can hold potty practice every two hours during the first day or two. However, you should only hold one practice a day until your child willingly stays in the bathroom for five minutes and sits on the potty for a minute without a struggle. Drop back to having him practice once or twice a day on workdays if necessary, and hold more whenever possible.

Ⓔ ALERT!

Try using an egg timer to time potty practice sessions. If your child is upset about having to practice, this helps focus your child's resentment away from you. Let it be the timer's fault that he has to sit on the potty for another few minutes. The egg timer never gets offended, and can take the heat!

Stress May Cause Setbacks

In truth, it is impossible to predict how long it will take for potty practice sessions to work their magic. Some children are still learning to remain seated and sit still long enough to have a chance to use the potty while others are completely trained. Even then, toddlers may have setbacks. During a particularly difficult period they may regress, have many accidents, or refuse to use the potty altogether, so that they must return to diapers or wear pull-ups for a time. The stress can be due to something in the child's environment—perhaps a change in daycare teachers or a divorce.

Stress can also be due to what is happening within the child. During that terribly-two-year-old stage when toddlers' desire to be grown up and in control collides with the reality of being young and helpless, potty refusals and accidents can become a real problem. Fortunately, retraining by putting the child back on a schedule of frequent practice sessions can be accomplished in short order once the child is back on an even keel. In the meantime, continue taking your child into the bathroom regularly even if he won't sit on the potty. Take a book for him to read and studiously ignore tantrums, but make sure he doesn't hurt himself by throwing himself about. Once he learns that he must remain in the bathroom until he's calmed down, his tantrums will subside. Soon after he's stopped struggling and remains calm, he'll be willing to sit on the potty for a bit. When he fully relaxes, he'll be able to use the potty if the timing of the practice sessions is right.

Trouble with the Next Step

A potential problem of this method is that some children get to the point of being virtually accident-free because they use the potty whenever their parent initiates a practice session at the right time, but they have trouble taking the next step: figuring out when they need to use the potty and going without a prompt. They can seem quite stuck for a while. If so, the motivational tricks and tactics described at the end of the chapter can help them complete training, as can the accident management strategies described in Chapter 8.

Getting Started

Use a potty chair rather than a potty seat. Tell your toddler that it is his, and set it in the play area so he can get used to it. Be sure that your child's bottom is covered the first few times he sits on it—the cold plastic can be so off-putting that some youngsters determine to make that first unpleasant surprise their last.

ESSENTIAL

> After your child relieves himself in his potty, sanitize it by wiping it down with a mild bleach solution before letting him play with it. To teach your child how to wipe himself correctly after using the potty, see the section on hygiene in Chapter 9.

If your child wants to sit on it bare-bottomed right away, suggest he touch the seat with his hands to test the temperature. If he thinks it is cold, the two of you can warm it with your hands for a minute first. First impressions are especially important for very timid, sensitive toddlers. Do what you can to make them good ones.

Keep the potty chair in the living room or your child's bedroom until he is comfortable with it, then start storing it in the bathroom. He can still take it out to play with it.

Demonstrating

During the first potty practice sessions, have your child accompany you to the bathroom while you use the toilet. It helps to pull down your underwear and actually use it, but if you are too uncomfortable, at least lift the lid and pretend. If your child senses your discomfort, he may conclude something scary is about to happen and feel afraid. Calmly explain, "Mommy is sitting on her big toilet. The potty is your little toilet."

It's fine if he wants to sit on his potty, but wait a few days until the novelty of being with you in the bathroom has worn off before suggesting it. If he sits on it with his clothes on, just say, "You're sitting on your little potty. Are you going to urinate or have a B.M.?" If he pretends to use it standing up "like Dad," explain that little boys have to sit down until they learn how. Nevertheless, don't squelch his desire to experiment. Let him take his time and get comfortable with the situation.

If Your Child Isn't Interested

If your child isn't interested in sitting on the potty after she has accompanied you to the bathroom several times, suggest that her doll or stuffed animal might want to go potty. Take a book or magazine with you and spend a few minutes reading and suggest she do the same. Stay relaxed so she can see that bathrooms and potties are nothing to be worried about. Spend a few minutes in the bathroom each day for a week before suggesting she sit on the potty bare-bottomed. Tell her to touch the potty seat first to make sure it isn't cold. Use your hands to warm the seat, and suggest she help you. Plan to move very slowly. In the end, you'll be glad you did!

 ALERT!

It helps if the same-sexed parent or older sibling can serve as a role model. It helps, too, if little boys can see an older male sit down to use the toilet as well as use it while standing.

If your child's reluctance to sit on the potty continues, she may have already absorbed some negative feelings about passing waste, be worried about what is expected of her, or be especially active and/or immature. Try taking the potty to the living room for potty practice. Have her sit on it fully clothed while you read her a story so she can start getting used to sitting on it. Push it up to the coffee table and let her sit on it to eat a picnic lunch in the living room. See if she wants to sit on it bare-bottomed while you read a story.

Teaching about Bowel Movements

If the idea of using the bathroom with your child present makes you too uncomfortable, invite him in afterward to give this lesson during a potty practice session. Point to your B.M. in the toilet and explain that it is "Mommy's B.M." or whatever word he is to use. After he is tired of looking at it, encourage him to wave and tell it "bye-bye" as you flush. Tell him that your body makes a B.M. every day and that you will show him again tomorrow. Encourage him to sit on his potty to see if he can make a B.M., too. If he brings up the subject of "Mommy's B.M." later in the day, keep a stiff upper lip even if it embarrasses you. Repeat the same procedure during a potty practice every day for about a week.

Meanwhile, whenever you notice that your child is having a B.M., bring it to his attention. As soon as he is finished, take him to the bathroom to remove his soiled diapers. Scrape the contents into the toilet while he watches, saying, "I'm putting your B.M. in the toilet just like Mommy's." When he is tired of looking at it, see if he wants to flush. Wave bye-bye together and explain that flushing is so "our B.M.s can be together." Tell him you'll put your B.M.s in the toilet again as soon as your body makes more, and that you'll put his B.M.s in the toilet again as soon as his body makes more. If he doesn't want to wave good-bye or looks even a little bit concerned, wait to flush until he leaves the room. Do this for about a week. The point is to try to stave off the intense "separation anxiety" so many toddlers develop. Many youngsters become so upset about their bowel movements being disposed of, they refuse to have a B.M. in the potty.

Teaching about Urination

Let your child accompany you to the bathroom for potty practice several days in a row and have her listen for when "Mommy is putting her urine in the toilet," or watch Daddy putting his in. Explain, "I am making urine now," in case she doesn't notice the sound. Tell her, "You put your urine in your diaper. Soon you will put it in the potty like me." Repeat the lesson whenever you discover a wet diaper. Be enthusiastic as you say, "They're wet because you put your urine in your diaper. Where does Mommy put hers? Yes! In her big potty! Where will you put yours someday? Yes! In your little potty," or some such. The goal is to help her to understand the basics of urination, that big people use the toilet, and that some day she will use it, too.

Feed water to a doll that wets and hold it over the toilet so your child can watch it urinate "in Mommy's potty." Give the doll another bottle and have her hold the doll over the potty, or hold it for her. Then make a tissue-paper diaper and put it on the doll with tape. Feed it another bottle, make it wet, and have your child feel its diaper as you explain, "It went pee-pee in its diaper." Later, when your child is drinking liquid, tell her that she will urinate soon. Just like the doll, she will wet her diaper. Explain that someday she will put her urine in her little potty like Mommy puts hers in her big potty.

Ⓔ FACT

Since birth your toddler has relieved himself automatically. Diapers hid the connection between sensations of fullness and wetting and soiling. He may need to see himself eliminating many times to recognize the sensations that signal he needs to go to the potty. You may need to remove his diaper and let him go about bare-bottomed so he can watch himself relieving himself.

Ask Your Child to Notify You

When your child is drinking, remind her about the doll that wet. Tell her that because she is drinking, she will soon wet her diaper. Ask her to tell you when that happens. From time to time ask, "Did the urine come yet?" If she says it did, check her diaper. If she correctly notified you, exclaim, "Yes! Your urine came! You put it in your diaper!" Be very happy indeed, if she can actually tell when she is urinating. If she was wrong, consider that disposable diapers may mask the sensations to the point that she can't tell what's going on. Switch to cloth diapers, which are less absorbent.

Ask your child often to tell you when her urine is coming, but if she doesn't like to have her diaper changed, postpone changing her. You want her to notice when "the urine is coming," not ignore it because she doesn't like being changed. If she tells you it is coming and her diaper is dry, say, "No, not yet. But soon it will come."

Pre-Potty Practice

After watching your child carefully and noting the times at which he eats and eliminates on a calendar, schedule one or more daily potty practices when your child is likely to need to have a bowel movement. Some children regularly have a bowel movement a half hour or so after eating, regardless of when they eat.

(E) **ESSENTIAL**

Punishing accidents by leaving your child in wet or messy clothes is abusive. The risk of rash and infection increases. In addition, he may become accustomed to wet diapers, so your punishment will backfire. Instead, teach your child to help with cleanup by taking a bath after soiling and by wiping up puddles with a sponge.

Several Daily Practices

Hold potty practice when you expect your child to have a bowel movement. If she is too irregular to predict, set up a regular schedule: When your schedule permits, hold potty practice first thing in the morning, shortly after breakfast, midmorning or immediately after a morning nap, shortly after lunch, midafternoon or immediately after her afternoon nap, shortly after dinner, and before bed. Although you should try to schedule practices around bowel movements, more frequent sessions give her more opportunities to urinate in the potty, too. Busy dual-income families and single working parents can ask day care providers to have their youngster spend five minutes in the bathroom at likely times or at regular two-hour intervals.

Do Your Best

If family schedules and unreliable caregivers make several daily practices impossible, do the best you can. Get up earlier in the morning so your child can practice first thing on awakening or after breakfast. Pick a time or two in the evening, perhaps after dinner or just before bed.

Ⓔ QUESTION?

My child sits on the potty very nicely but doesn't use it. What is the problem?
Being able to use the potty isn't just a question of sitting on it at the right time. Children must have waste in their systems, and they must be relaxed enough for their sphincters to open up so the waste can flow out.

If you can only manage once or twice a day during the work week, remember that while toddlers can learn to remain seated, relax, and use the potty, it will take them much longer to develop the habit of going to the potty each and every time they need to relieve themselves. Try putting the potty chair in the living room so your child can spend more time sitting on it while he is playing at a small desk, watching a video, or listening to a story. Have him wear pull-ups so he can easily use the potty any time he wants to, and provide a reward whenever he does use it. Otherwise, try to finish potty training during a week-long stay-at-home vacation when your schedule allows you to hold practices once every two hours.

Beginning Potty Practice

When your child doesn't object to sitting on the potty without a diaper, begin generating excitement for the big event. Announce that he will wear pull-ups and learn to use the potty just like Mommy/Daddy/big brother/big sister and all the big kids at day care. Choose a time when he is in a good mood, rested, and healthy.

Take him to the bathroom shortly before you expect him to have a bowel movement and close the door. Put a small piece of toilet paper in the potty so that if he urinates just a tiny bit, you will be able to tell by looking at the paper and can congratulate him. Show him how to pull his pants and pull-ups down to his ankles, bending at the knees so he doesn't fall. Have him sit all the way back on the potty chair with the legs slightly spread so you can see and point out what is happening if he begins urinating.

(E) FACT

The advantage to timing potty practice sessions to coincide with bowel movements is that when the anal sphincter opens to pass stool, the urinary sphincter opens, too. Any urine in the bladder is passed when the bowel movement takes place. Hence, as tots learn to use the potty for bowel movements, they practice urinating in the potty, too.

If He Wants to Stand

If he wants to use the potty standing up, explain that big boys and Daddies sit to have B.M.s and stand up to urinate, and that he can stand, too, after he learns to use it sitting down. Don't press him, though. He is likely to be more excited than usual, which may make sitting extra hard. Encourage him to focus on his physical sensations by telling him to let you know when he feels like his urine or B.M. is wanting to come out. Children also urinate when they have bowel movements, so tell him to sit down on the potty fast and hold his penis down if a bowel movement starts. However, moving too fast could cause him to bump a splash guard, which hurts. Remove it to guard against a painful accident.

Helping Your Child

Show him how to "try" by grunting and acting as if you're straining to have a bowel movement. However, many toddlers tense their sphincter muscles in the process, so "trying" may not work. Run some water in the sink or dip his hands in a bowl of tepid water. It may be an old wives' tale, but lots of old wives say it stimulates urination! Teach him to relax by closing your eyes, taking slow, deep breaths, and telling him to do the same. If he wanders, tell him to stay near the potty so he can sit down when he needs to use it. Don't press him to remain seated—he may be too tense to relieve himself anyway.

Gotta Go!

If your child shows signs that a bowel movement is starting or if he begins urinating, guide him to the potty and encourage him to sit down. If he gets upset, back off and let the accident happen. He will need to get comfortable more gradually. If he does use the potty, be enthusiastic so he can appreciate that he has done something important.

Ⓔ ALERT!

End each potty practice session by having your child wash his hands whether or not he used the potty. This is the way to start developing the hand-washing habit!

Show him how much toilet paper to use and how to tear it off. Help him wipe, empty the potty bowl, flush, rinse the bowl, put it back in the potty chair, and wash his hands. Even if he only urinated, let him use toilet paper. Toddlers find these after-potty tasks the best rewards of all. Don't view them as chores and your child won't, either.

Recognizing the Sensations

If your child begins urinating during potty practice and doesn't even notice, dig in for a long haul. He may need a lot of help from you to recognize the sensations. Calmly point out what is happening. Plan to take him outside on a warm day or spend a morning in the kitchen with him bare-bottomed so he can observe himself in the act of urinating. Switch to cloth diapers. Disposables may have kept him from noticing when he passes waste.

First "Success"

If your child begins eliminating unexpectedly when he isn't sitting on the potty, tell him to try to stop. Few toddlers know how to stop once they've started, but at least he'll know it's possible, and it's important to start teaching the lesson that he should go to the potty whenever he is passing waste. If he does stop, say, "Good boy!" and guide him to the potty fast.

Have an extra bowl within easy reach so that if he has the usual toddler reaction of standing still and watching himself urinate, you can try to catch some urine in the extra bowl and pour it into his potty bowl to show him where it's supposed to go. If you can't catch any in a bowl, get a very wet sponge or soaking wet washcloth when he finishes urinating, wipe up some urine with the sponge, and show him how to squeeze some into his potty. Be enthusiastic as you say something like, "Your urine came out and you put it in the potty where it belongs!" When he is through admiring it, help him pour it into the toilet "so it can go bye-bye with Mama's urine." Invite him to flush, but if he doesn't respond, flush after he has left the room. The violence of the swirling water upsets many children.

Ⓔ ESSENTIAL

Until using the potty has become a habit, your child must constantly keep tabs on the fullness of her bladder and bowel. Such extended concentration is exhausting. Don't be surprised if she is especially cranky and tired. Try to scale back your expectations in other areas, and pour on the TLC!

He's Learning!

Your child has now been through the entire process and should have a better idea as to what's involved even if he didn't have a bowel movement and didn't make it to the potty when he urinated. Hold practice sessions regularly, about once every two hours, and try to have him sit on the potty for five minutes each time.

When he notifies you that he needs to use the potty or starts taking himself, you may not need to hold regular practice sessions unless he gets distracted and doesn't go when there are more fun things to do. Help him share the good news that he's starting to learn to use the potty with a friend or family member. He's earned his bragging rights!

If Nothing Happens

If your child doesn't urinate or have a bowel movement during his first potty practice session, he either didn't need to use it or was too tense to release waste. Begin holding regular potty practice sessions timed to coincide with when you expect he might need to go, and have him spend three to five minutes practicing relaxing.

If he protests strongly about having to stay in the bathroom, remain calm and let the tantrum run its course—which may mean you end up in the bathroom for a very long time. Don't have a tantrum, too, by yelling or getting upset. Don't let him leave the bathroom until he is completely calm (unless you're losing it and need a break). Try to end each upsetting session on a positive note: "This was hard, but you calmed down!" After a tantrum, give him the rest of the day to recover before having another practice. After two or three tantrums to learn that noisy upset won't end a potty practice session, things get easier.

Even if your timing is good and your child remains seated on the potty during the practices, he may still be too tense to eliminate. Don't be surprised if he soils or wets as soon as he stands up or shortly after the practice session ends and his diaper is back on. This is normal. The sphincter won't open until he relaxes. Tell him he can try again later, clean him up, wait about two hours, and hold another potty practice. Until he can comfortably remain seated for five minutes, devote the sessions to helping him relax.

 FACT

> Show your toddler boy how to hold his penis down to direct the stream of urine. Help him remember to concentrate by giving positive feedback: "You're getting the urine in the potty! Very good!" When he forgets, give him a sponge to help clean up, and give him positive feedback for that, too: "Great! You're cleaning the splashes!"

If she uses the potty, have her empty and rinse the potty bowl and wash her hands. If she has an accident shortly before a practice session, hold it anyway if you think she would benefit from practicing sitting on the potty and relaxing.

Relaxation Training

Whenever your child has a potty practice session, tell her that she must relax before she can use the potty. Keep your focus positive by noting anything she does *right* as she works on relaxing: "Your arms are resting now. That's a good way to relax," or "You're sitting nicely." If she swings her legs, wait until she stops swinging them and then tell her that you're glad she's holding them still. Show her how to relax while sitting on the potty by closing your eyes and breathing deeply as you sit on the toilet.

Put your arm on her fidgety hands to show her how to hold still, and say, "Yes! That's the way to sit still." It may be tempting to strap your little busy bee to the potty chair to keep her there, but that is abusive! Keeping her in wet or soiled pants as punishment teaches nothing and is abusive, too.

Help her relax by making the time pleasant, too. Sit next to her on the floor while she sits on the potty and read her a book, sing a song together, or recite nursery rhymes. Avoid rowdy play. Eventually you want her to sit by herself without needing to be entertained, but distracting her at the outset by making the time pleasant will help her relax. Children have a hard time relaxing and sitting still if they have a lot of pent-up energy. Provide time for active play before each potty practice session.

Clothing

It's generally too messy to let children wear underpants until they use the potty at least half of the time, but the problem with diapers is that children can't get them off easily to use the potty by themselves. By having your child put on her pull-ups or underpants for each potty practice, she can practice pulling them down before sitting on the potty and pulling them back up at the end of the session. You can put her diaper back on before sending her off to play. However, some toddlers can more easily remember to go to the potty when wearing cloth pull-ups or underpants because they are so aware of being in big-girl clothes. By wearing cloth they can immediately tell when they've had an accident, so after an accident or two many children learn to get themselves to the potty in time. It's worth a try. If your child is having too many accidents to make it practical for her to wear underpants outside of potty practice sessions, you can solve the problem by putting her in diapers or putting a waterproof cover over underpants. A compromise for a child who insists on wearing underpants is to let her wear them as long as she keeps them clean and dry. Put her in diapers after each accident, then reward her for using the potty by letting her change into underpants afterward.

(E) ESSENTIAL

Have your child prepare for potty practice by dancing, running, or engaging in other vigorous play to work off energy. Provide a special toy or book that invites quiet, relaxed play and designate it for use during potty practice sessions only. That can boost motivation to practice and lessen tots' resistance to sitting on the potty.

Small Rewards

Small rewards help motivate children to remain seated—provided that the rewards are easy for them to earn. Set up your youngster to succeed, never to fail. Give a sticker for staying seated for just one or two minutes at first, and slowly work up to five minutes. Only reward real successes—don't break down and give her a reward because she's sad—but the accomplishments can be very small ones.

Track Progress

Once your child can relax on the potty, he should be able to have bowel movements during potty practice if your timing is right. With more frequent practices timed to his patterns of urinating, he should be able to make rapid progress. Track his progress on a calendar by noting the times he uses the potty and have him affix a sticker to the calendar as a reward. You might provide a very special sticker each time he goes to the potty outside of a scheduled session, too. Write down the time of each accident so you can keep track and do a better job of timing his practice sessions.

Taking Initiative

Be sure your child understands that if he goes potty by himself, he won't need his regular potty practice session. Then, when the scheduled time for a practice session has arrived, reinforce his accomplishment by announcing, "It's time for potty practice, but you went potty by yourself so you can keep on playing. You don't need to practice."

A Common Problem

Some children become very good at using the potty during regularly scheduled practice sessions. The problem is, they only use it when their parent takes them to the bathroom. Otherwise, they relieve themselves at will. Suggestions that they take themselves when they need to go potty seem to fall on deaf ears. Don't think your child is being defiant! The sensation of a diaper, pull-ups, or underwear triggers the old habit of passing waste without thinking. After each accident they may feel very repentant but not improve.

 ALERT!

If your child complies with potty practice rules but won't go to the potty on his own, try the Tickle Game or Beat the Clock (Chapter 9) to help her understand what you expect and encourage her to take initiative.

A Solution

Some children have difficulty connecting the sensation of a full bladder or bowel with the waste that flows from the body. One solution is to have your child go bare-bottomed for a day to help her comprehend this all-important connection. Keep the potty close by and see if she can use it without having to be told. Ask, "Do you need to use the potty?" if you see signs that she needs to relieve herself, but don't press her to sit on it. Her first response may well be to have an accident. If so, she probably hasn't made the connection between the sensation of fullness and passing waste. Tell her to run to the potty the next time she feels "the urine or B.M. wanting to come." Repeat this procedure as often as necessary so she can learn to make the connection. Continue to encourage her to sit on the potty when she feels her urine coming.

In the meantime, give her a sponge so she can start learning to clean up, but don't insist that she actually do any work. If she does go potty by herself or asks to be taken even once as her day of going bare-bottomed wears on, this could be a major turning point. Be enthusiastic and reward her. Try to keep her bottoms off for the rest of the day, and let her go bare-bottomed for the next few days to help the habit develop of going to the potty each and every time.

Reconditioning

If your child continues to have one accident after the next while she is bare-bottomed, don't assume the problem is lack of motivation. Many parents condition their babies only to relieve themselves when they have something covering their bottoms. You may have done this by shrieking when you unexpectedly got sprayed while changing a diaper, or by yelling for your baby to stop urinating when her diaper was off. If a baby is startled by the parent's shrieks and yells, the sphincter clamps shut. When urination stops, the upsetting noise the parent was making stops, too. Afterward, whenever the baby's diaper is off or her bottom is bare, the sphincters tighten to contain waste inside the body in order to prevent any more of those startling shrieks and yells. The sphincters only relax enough for waste to be released in two situations: when the diaper or underpants are on, or when the pressure of an overly full bladder and/or bowel suddenly forces them open. The result is lots of accidents. The solution is to re-condition the sphincters. The following tricks and tactics can help.

 FACT

> Recondition sphincters that have been conditioned to remain shut whenever your child's bottom is bare by creating a distraction to "confuse" them. Do that by singing or playing with him while he is sitting on the potty. Alternatively, encourage your child to fight the sphincters' tendency to close by increasing his motivation to use the potty so much that he consciously forces them open.

Tricks and Tactics

It's amazing how a single trick can capture toddlers' imagination and provide a permanent motivational fix. In addition, these tactics can help recondition the sphincters so they can open instead of remaining closed as long as possible whenever your child's bottom is bare.

Sail the ping-pong ball. Drop a ping-pong ball in the toilet bowl and let toddler boys sail it as they spray. It will help them learn to aim before firing. Wash your hands after retrieving it!

Bull's eye. Draw a magic marker target on a piece of tissue paper and drop it in the potty or toilet bowl and see if your little boy can score a hit. Your little girl may get a kick out of this kind of target practice, too, even if she can't see what she's doing.

Sink or swim? Float a piece of paper towel in the toilet bowl and see if your toddler can sink it. Improve his aim by using progressively smaller pieces.

Firefighter. Suggest your toddler don his firefighter hat and douse the imaginary blaze raging in the toilet with his urine. That means, of course, that he will have to go fast if he's to save the house from ruin. Next time he's wiggling about, don't yell, "Go to the potty *now*!" Just yell, "*Fire!*"

Gardener. Paint flowers inside the potty bowl or affix stickers featuring flowers. Alternatively, cut the flower designs off of printed paper towels and drop them into the toilet. Then, declare the "garden" in need of a sprinkle. If it's time to have a bowel movement, what the heck? Suggest the flowers need to be fertilized!

Sweeter than roses. Tell your child how nice she smells now that she's used the potty and kept her pants clean. To drive home the message, squirt her with a dollop of cologne. Little boys love this, too.

Meet the Lump family. Are her B.M.s big enough to be the "daddies," small enough to be the "children," or the right size to count as "mommies"? Have her decide. Then she can tuck them in for the night by flushing.

Toilet rainbows. Add a few drops of blue food coloring in the toilet bowl (or a bit of water and food coloring to the potty bowl) so your child can delight in watching it turn green when he adds yellow urine. Or color the water red so she can turn it orange.

Bare bottomed. Underwear feels enough like diapers to some children that they forget they're wearing them. The old habit kicks in and they do what they've done since the day they were born: relieve themselves without pausing to consider. Remove it, and the strange sensation of nakedness serves as an on-going reminder to use the potty, even if they are still wearing a dress or pants. After a few days of constant awareness, they can wear underwear again without forgetting.

High fashion. The chance to don special "big boy" or "big girl" pull-ups or underpants can be exciting. The downside is that accidents can be very messy and require a complete change of clothes. Encourage your child to concentrate by setting the rule up front: "You can wear your underpants when you're ready to use the potty." Place them out of reach but within view, such as on top of a dresser, and wait for your child to ask to wear them. Alternatively, offer them as a reward: Every time your child uses the potty, she can wear them until she has an accident.

Big is better! Rewards must be immediate to be effective, but sometimes the visual reward of a check mark or sticker on a calendar for each dry day is a potent incentive—especially if a week's worth of checks can be exchanged for a very special toy or outing. Thinking so far ahead may be beyond most toddlers, but one four-year-old stayed dry from the day his parents promised to buy the antique Civil War sword he was determined to have decorating the wall of his bedroom. Another went the distance for a Michael Jackson CD. Inappropriate toddler rewards? Perhaps, but what the heck? They worked.

Here, there, and (almost) everywhere! Have your child experiment with urinating in interesting containers—a bucket, jar, tin can, cup, pan, bowl, flowerpot, hole in the ground, etc. This is a great potty training tension reliever, and can help them overcome the idea that the one and only place to urinate is at home in their very own potty. Public restrooms may then be okay, too.

Move it! Nowhere is it written that a child must go to the potty. The potty can just as easily go to your child. Suggest he move it into the play area, put it in his bedroom at night, set it in the kitchen during meals. Once he gets in the habit of seeking it out when he needs it, those few extra steps won't be such a bother. Try a pet pad under the potty seat in a carpeted room. It helps soak up spills and splashes.

The easy chair. Some potties are comfy, with lids that close, tall backs, and arm rests. Why not move it into the living room so your child can relax on it while watching TV? Of course, TV-watching isn't good for toddlers, and they're *never* supposed to do it. But if they are, maybe they can sit on the potty with their pants down and the lid up and reap a small benefit.

Rewards

Until children develop the habit of using the potty, it is parents who reap the rewards. Children lose the one-on-one time they spent being changed. They trade the carefree days of diapers for having to monitor the state of their bladder at every moment. They have to drop what they're doing and run to the potty all day long. Small presents, hugs, and affection can focus your child's attention on a task he could care less about, thus helping to keep his motivation high enough for long enough so that the potty-going habit can be established. Rewards can also keep the tone of potty training positive and upbeat.

 ALERT!

Although it's preferable to have children strive to please parents rather than to obtain treats and goodies, the mere act of handing over a reward helps parents to stay involved and express approval.

Sweet Rewards

Candy is not the sort of reward health-conscious parents want to give, but it may be a great way to motivate your child. If stickers and small toys don't work or are too expensive, try for something like a raisin, fish cracker, or tidbit of whole grain cereal before moving to an M&M or tidbit of sugary cereal. Dole one out each time your child uses the potty or completes a specific task that is giving him problems, such as going to the potty without a prompt or reminder, wiping himself after bowel movements, keeping urine in the potty, wiping splashes from the sink after hand washing, or flushing the toilet.

If your child has really big problems with one particular task, provide a more enticing reward to help him focus on the area he finds difficult and to motivate him to struggle on. For instance, if he sometimes gets himself to the potty to urinate but never for a B.M., give one piece for the former and buy him a Porsche for the latter. Well, maybe just a replica. Be sure to supply other caregivers with a stock of rewards, coordinate so you're on the same page, keep each other informed of progress and problems, and discuss changes in advance.

Ⓔ QUESTION?

My child doesn't care about praise or rewards. What's wrong? What can I do?
Probably potty training feels far too overwhelming. Quit for a month, start over more gradually, and reward even tiny successes.

Consistency

Too many changes in reward systems can confuse kiddies, so try to think things through in advance. Clearly communicate what your child must do to earn a reward, and exactly what the reward will be. Consider carefully exactly what will count as a success. Sitting still for three minutes? Going to the potty with or without a reminder? Urinating in the potty? Or will he be rewarded for every hour that he keeps his diapers dry? If so, that could add up to a lot of M&Ms! Yet rewarding children for staying clean and dry is definitely an excellent idea.

It's okay to gradually increase the requirements for

earning a reward since toddlers can generally comprehend them. For instance, after he is urinating and having B.M.s in the potty without a problem, the next step is teaching responsibility, so you might require him to complete all toileting tasks to receive a reward: empty the potty bowl, flush the toilet, dispose of toilet paper scraps, wipe up splashes, wash and dry hands, etc.

Reward programs bog down when the rules keep changing or are overly complicated: No more candy for urinating in the potty, only a sticker; candy is only for a B.M. but you can have two pieces instead of one and if you sit still you get a penny. Don't focus on more than two issues at a time, and even that may be too much. Test your child's understanding: "What do you get for urinating in the potty?" and "What do you get for sitting on the potty when a B.M. is coming?" If he can't answer, your reward system won't mean anything to him.

For starters, keep the bag of M&Ms (or whatever) close to the potty but out of reach, accompany your child to the bathroom, and give food rewards by popping them right into his mouth and letting him know what he did right. Otherwise, hand him his food reward when he has finished wiping and flushing and, most importantly, washing his hands. He should never touch food after using the bathroom until his hands are washed.

Gradually separate the candy from the praise by confining yourself to saying what he did right as you give him the reward. Choose other times to mention how pleased you are with the way he's been handling the potty. A good time to make a positive comment might be when you think that he needs to use the potty but isn't moving in that direction: "You've been so good about going to the potty! You haven't had an accident all day." If he doesn't respond to your prompt, let the accident happen. He won't learn to take responsibility if you take it for him! Afterward, let him help clean up while you figure out where to get the money for new carpeting when he is finally trained.

Taking More Responsibility

Let your child gradually take more responsibility by giving less direction and fewer prompts as to what to do next. Instead of standing over him to tell him what to do next in the bathroom, wait until he considers himself finished, then tell him what still needs to be done. After he empties the potty bowl, flushes the toilet, and wipes up splashes from the floor, have him rewash his hands before giving the reward.

Phasing Out Rewards

While parents are usually careful to praise and reward first potty successes, enthusiasm typically wanes long before children achieve that all-important goal of going to the potty each and every time they need to. Parents tire of having to drop what they are doing to "watch me go!" or "see what I did!" They make excuses so as not to have to participate and become lack-adaisical as they distractedly mutter, "That's great."

Soon their own disinterest is reflected in their child's waning attention to remaining accident-free. He's as enthusiastic about going to the potty as the parent is about helping him.

The solution is to remain involved as long as your child needs encouragement to keep going, then phase out your involvement gradually, but only after he is fully trained.

1. Stay with him in the bathroom the whole time and give him a reward.
2. Help him get started in the bathroom, leave, go back in, give him a reward.
3. Tell him to go on ahead, join him in the bathroom a minute later, give him a reward.
4. Tell him to call you when he's finished in the bathroom, join him there, do a bathroom inspection, check his hands, and give him a reward.
5. Tell him to come find you when he's finished in the bathroom, check his hands, then give him a reward.

When your child uses the potty regularly for a week without prompts or reminders, move the rewards to the kitchen. Have him go to the potty by himself and come to you afterward to collect. Check his hands. If they're not clean, send him back. Check them again when he returns, then give him his due.

The first time your child forgets to come ask for his reward, you'll know he's nearing the finish line. Most children then forget with increasing frequency. You can "help" by conversing on another subject after she emerges from the bathroom but before she asks for her reward. But if she does ask for it, give it immediately! A deal's a deal!

 FACT

> When toddlers are conflicted about independence, praise can increase power struggles. Instead of trying to get a surly rebel to "do it for Mom," let him just do it for the reward.

Try offering a choice in hopes of being able to provide rewards you feel better about giving: An M&M or a sticker? An M&M or a story? An M&M or a trip to the park? An M&M or a trip to the store after lunch to buy new underwear? An M&M or a ride on the mechanical horse at the grocery store after dinner? An M&M or a chance to fingerpaint later in the day? To earn a delayed reward, add that she must not wet or soil beforehand or the deal is off.

M&Ms Forever

When it comes to potty training, parents tend to imagine the worst, fearing they'll be doling out M&Ms and stickers forever. It just doesn't work out that way. Nevertheless, if your child has been fully trained for quite some time but isn't about to forget to collect his piece of candy after every success, it's time for the healthy teeth cure: Since candy is bad for his teeth he must brush every time after eating his M&M. If he's willing to brush after each sweet reward, so be it. Don't expect a toddler to do a good job of brushing, but do expect him to put forth a real effort. With practice he'll improve.

Finally, cut out other desserts, snacks, and sodas to balance out his diet. Then forget the whole thing. A small daily dose of M&Ms is a bargain if it buys a potty trained child who brushes his teeth six or seven times a day!

Chapter 6
Fast-Track Toddler Method

For some families, this intensive approach is ideal—it is fast and painless. Given that your child is doing in a day what many toddlers take months to accomplish, be sure your child has the physical, cognitive, emotional, and social skills to succeed before you try it. Be sure that you can remain calm, too. A bad potty training experience can create a setback.

Toilet Training in Less Than a Day

Children who are twenty months and older can be potty trained with amazing speed. The method for toilet training in less than a day developed by Nathan Azrin and Richard Foxx and described in their book *Toilet Training in Less Than a Day* has become a classic. This fast-track method has a number of components.

- Feed your child lots of liquids so she can practice using the potty often during a short period of time.
- Demonstrate the process using a doll that wets.
- Manually guide your child to ensure she understands and follows directions.
- Teach self-affirmations to instill confidence and boost motivation.
- Give drinks and snacks as rewards to boost motivation and increase urination.
- Have your child practice going to the potty after accidents, so she learns to go without delay when the need arises in the future.

Mixed Reactions

Reactions to this method are mixed. Lots of parents find it easy and enjoyable, and have had success with it after other methods failed. Many parents find the process considerably more challenging, but are still delighted with the speedy results. However, some parents reported that their children became so upset, they had to abandon potty training altogether and wait a month before starting over with a different method. Do not hesitate to stop if you think it is too trying!

It's Not for Everyone

Parents accustomed to the "time out" method may find this fast-track method is out of step with their usual approach to resolving parent/child conflicts. Although "time out" is supposed to provide a brief cooling off period so children can face a problem calmly, many parents consider the problem over and done with once the child settles down. Hence, many parents lack experience teaching children to comply with rules and have a hard time confronting uncooperative youngsters. Today's children have less experience complying with parental demands than youngsters of generations past.

Unless parents have good emotional control, they may become overwhelmed to the point that they lash out and become abusive. The resulting psychological trauma can be serious, setting back overall emotional development as well as potty training. Chronic problems with soiling and wetting may be the tragic result. Therefore, parents should end the lessons immediately if they experience an urge to lash out.

Before You Begin

Although children are continuously rewarded when they cooperate and must not be punished in any way, this program is very strict. Being strict is different from getting angry and punishing, however. Try to decide in advance whether you will have the patience to manage the situation calmly, yet firmly, if your child resists.

You may have to steer your youngster to the potty and apply gentle pressure to get him to sit down if he won't comply voluntarily. Even if you are guiding a balky youngster back to the potty and sitting him down for the tenth time in two minutes, you must not lose patience or use more force than absolutely necessary, no matter that you are very frustrated. Instead, you must give continuous feedback and praise. For instance, say, "Good boy! You are going to the bathroom," as you steer him there, and, "Yes, you are sitting down, that's good!" as you apply light pressure to his shoulders. If your child does not comply with an instruction, act as though he simply didn't understand you, even if you think he is being stubborn.

Ⓔ ALERT!

Punishing a child for potty accidents and refusals can cause psychological trauma and set back overall emotional development as well as potty training efforts. Chronic problems with soiling and wetting may be the tragic result. Be kind!

You must also be careful to give only one instruction at a time. Never issue a second instruction until your child completes the first. Provide lots of praise, hugs, pats, and smiles when he is learning something new or doing something difficult. However, praise becomes meaningless, even offensive, when given for something that posed no challenge. So drop back to a smile or nod when your child complies readily or is doing something easy. Continue to praise your child for having dry pants. Keeping them dry may remain a challenge for him for quite some time.

Toddler Readiness

For this method to work, your toddler must already stay dry for several hours at a time, walk unassisted, and have enough motor coordination to raise and lower her pants. She must be able to imitate simple movements, and learn by watching. She must be willing and able to comply with the following simple commands:

- Come when called.
- Pick up a toy when told to do so.
- Bring a familiar object such as a doll, book, or article of clothing when instructed.
- Walk to a bedroom or other room of the house when instructed.
- Place one object inside of another when directed.
- Remain seated when requested to do so.

Toddlers are never completely reliable about doing as they are told, and even typically cooperative youngsters can suddenly refuse to mind during potty training. Either your child must have a basic desire to please you or you must be exceptionally patient.

Training Preparations

Because this training program is intensive, gather everything you will need in advance. The last thing you want is to derail training by running out of the materials necessary to make this method work. You will need the following supplies:

❑ **A doll that wets, doll bottle, and doll underpants.** Children will learn the procedures and practice them with the doll.

❑ **Your child's favorite beverages in a variety of flavors.** To ensure that youngsters get to use the potty often in a short period of time, they need to drink large quantities of liquids. Stock up on a variety of your child's favorite beverages so when she tires of one you may encourage her to drink another.

❑ **Several kinds of salty snacks, such as chips, crackers, pretzels, and peanuts.** Salt increases thirst, so stock up on several kinds of your child's favorite salty foods. Don't rely on salted vegetable sticks, which are too filling.

❑ **Underpants.** Cloth underpants will help you and your child know when she is wet. The underpants should be several sizes too large so the child can pull them down quickly.

❏ **A potty chair.** It is helpful, though not essential, to use a chair that signals when urination begins.

Begin on a day when your child is healthy and well rested. Encourage him to drink a lot at breakfast, and try to keep him drinking at least one cup per hour throughout training so he will urinate about once every fifteen minutes. Provide salty snacks to increase thirst. Snacks and drinks double as rewards, so reward often! Make arrangements for brothers and sisters to be gone for the day. Turn the TV and radio off and keep the answering machine on throughout training.

Doll Demonstration

Put on the doll's underwear, feed it a bottle of water, and then explain that the doll has to urinate. Give your child the following instructions.

1. "Take the doll to the potty."
2. "Take off her pants."
3. "Sit her on the potty."
4. "Look between her legs."

Make the doll release water, and point out what is happening by exclaiming, "Look! The doll is urinating in the potty!" Tell your child to praise it and reward it with a pretend snack or sip of juice so he understands that using the potty is a good thing. He will be similarly praised and rewarded when he uses the potty.

Next, help your child remove the potty bowl, empty it into the toilet, flush, and return the bowl to the potty. Provide lots of verbal feedback, encouragement, and manual guidance to familiarize him with the words and phrases and keep him moving in the right direction. Continuously describe what is happening: "You're carrying dolly's urine to the toilet. You're putting dolly's urine in the toilet. You're flushing the toilet." You'll expect him to do these things after he uses the potty, too.

Ⓔ ESSENTIAL

Most training methods emphasize using the potty, but the fast-track method emphasizes keeping pants clean and dry. Show your child how to feel the crotch to see if his pants are wet or dry, and have him check them every few minutes.

Afterward, put dry pants on the doll. Have your child check its pants and praise it for being dry. Then have him check his own pants. If they are dry, give him a sip of a drink he likes as a reward. If they are wet but he says, "Dry!" say, "No, they're wet." If he says, "Wet!" say, "That's right, they're wet." Tell him you will teach him to use the potty like the doll, then change him.

Spill water on the doll's pants when your child isn't looking. Have him check its pants again and tell the doll, "No, big boys and girls don't wet their pants." Do not let him punish the doll. Tell him that it needs to practice using the potty.

ⒺESSENTIAL

> After each accident, your child will be required to practice getting to and using the potty five times. She will hurry to the potty, remove her pants, sit down for two seconds, pull her pants up, and hurry back to where she had the accident. Be forewarned: She probably won't like practicing, and might get upset.

As your child hurries the doll back and forth to the potty from where it had the "accident" again and again, placing it on the potty briefly each time, he learns what he must do when he has an accident. He needs to understand that practicing going to the potty fast is the way to learn not to have accidents.

Affirmations

Self-affirmations create a positive mindset. They highlight the advantages of using the potty and help youngsters state, to themselves or aloud, their intention to be successful. Teach your child by saying, "Daddy will be glad when you urinate in the potty. Will you urinate in the potty?" and encourage your child to say "yes" or nod. Say, "Big boys don't wet their pants. Are you going to wet your pants?" and encourage your child to say "no" or shake his head. Even if he does not respond, hopefully he will think the answers. You must repeat such statements and questions often before your child will begin repeating them to himself. It's hard to predict exactly what statement will strike a chord with a particular child, so vary them.

- "Uncle Mark goes to the potty by himself. Will you go to the potty by yourself like Uncle Mark?"
- "Big boys wear underpants, not diapers. Are you a big boy?"
- "Will Mama give you some chips when you urinate in the potty?"
- "Daddy doesn't wet his pants. Will you wet your pants?"
- "Mama doesn't like wet diapers. Will you keep your pants dry?"
- "Are you going to wet your pants?"

If your child says "yes" to the last statement, answer, "No, you are a big boy. You're going to wear pants like Daddy," or something along those lines.

Potty Practice

During potty practice, your child learns to walk to the potty chair, lower his pants, sit down, relax for up to ten minutes, get up, and pull his pants up. Try to get your child to relax while sitting on the potty so he can actually use it. The first time he urinates in the potty is likely to be because he has been drinking a lot and is now sitting on the potty. He may not realize what happened, so watch carefully and praise him when he uses it.

 FACT

> Potty bowls with moisture sensors play a tune so you can tell when your child urinates. If your child's potty does not have this feature, have your child spread her legs a bit. Sit on the floor and watch carefully so you can point out when she urinates, praise her, and give a reward.

After ten minutes of trying to get him to remain seated and relax, give him a break. If he did not urinate, watch him carefully. Tell him to go to the potty quickly if you think he may have to relieve himself.

Repeat the cycle of sitting on the potty and taking a break until he urinates in the potty for the first time. Give him a sip and salty snack as a reward, then show him how to wipe, raise his pants, empty the potty bowl, flush, rinse the potty bowl, replace it on the potty chair, and wash his hands before sending him on break. Now you know he can relax on the potty enough to be able to use it. Thereafter, he only needs to sit on the potty for five minutes at most and spend the rest of his time, about ten minutes, on break.

Learning to Relax

Although you may be anxious for your child to urinate in the potty, telling him to "try" probably won't help because he will tense up. Instead, teach him to relax while he is sitting. Most little ones would have to be forced to remain seated for longer than a minute or two, and struggles don't promote relaxation! Encourage him when he briefly sits by saying, "Good! You're sitting still." For little wrigglers, periods of decreased movement may be rare indeed, so observe carefully and comment fast!

Breaks

Breaks are important so your child learns to stop playing and go to the potty when told. Anytime he appears to need to use the potty while on break, send him to the potty immediately. Be enthusiastic. Say, "It looks like you need to urinate! Great! Go to the potty quickly! Hurry!" but do not argue about it. If he has an accident but has not yet managed to urinate in the potty, say, "Don't worry. I'm going to teach you to use the potty," and change his wet clothing. If he is on break and goes to the potty without being told, praise him heartily! He understands what he's supposed to do, and he did it!

If your child has an accident while on break, change him and wait a few minutes before telling him to sit on the potty again. There is no point in having him sit on the potty when you know he doesn't need to use it. After he has used the potty once, start dealing with accidents directly.

Potty Practice Prompts

Another goal of the potty practice sessions is to teach children to walk to the potty without being prompted. Start the first two or three potty practice sessions by saying, "Go to the potty." If your child so much as looks in the right direction, say, "That's right. Go to the potty." Provide ongoing verbal feedback even if a tantrum ensues. Gently grasp your youngster's shoulders and steer her to the potty, remove her pants, sit her down briefly, and put her pants back on while saying, "Yes, you're practicing going to the potty. I'm taking off your pants. You're sitting down. I'm putting your pants back on. Very good! You went to the potty!"

E **ESSENTIAL**

> Comfort an upset child by reassuring him that going to the potty will get easier and he will have fewer accidents after he learns to hurry to the potty and get his pants down fast. Practice really does make perfect!

Do not insist an upset child remain seated on the potty for more than a few seconds. She cannot urinate unless she's relaxed. If the tantrum is intense, wait until it's over before continuing potty practices. Forge ahead as soon as your child calms down, even though you will probably have another tantrum on your hands.

Resistance may be the same or greater after the first tantrum. Forge ahead again when your child calms down a second time, and compliance should be better. Often you will notice a dramatic improvement after two tumultuous practice sessions. Almost every child settles down after the third tantrum.

If at any point during a potty practice period your child walks to the potty and sits down without being prompted, express your delight in this big accomplishment!

Reducing Prompts

After a child complies readily when told to go to the potty during one practice session, switch to a gentler prompt for the next one. For instance, ask, "Do you want to go to the potty?" instead of telling your child to go to the potty. Go back to the firmer "Go to the potty" statement if your child does not comply when you ask him if he needs to go.

Once your child responds to the general prompt, "Do you want to go to the potty?" by going, tell her to show you where she urinates. If she points to the potty, you can safely assume she understands its purpose, so if she has also urinated in the potty at least one time, potty practice ends. If she does not point to the potty, hold more potty practice sessions, alternating with breaks until she goes to the potty when told and indicates that she understands that she is to urinate there.

Handling Accidents

Even if your child uses the potty the first time she sits on it, sooner or later an accident is bound to occur. Most youngsters think that once training is over, they can go back to wetting in their clothes. Perhaps they do not understand that they are supposed to keep using the potty, or they misjudge how long it takes to get to the potty and get their pants down, or maybe they just don't feel like using it. After your child has urinated in the potty one time, she does understand what she's supposed to do, so respond to accidents after that point by saying that they are unacceptable. Some youngsters are highly sensitive, so a little disapproval goes a long way. Be firm when you say, "No! Don't wet your pants!" but do not yell.

 ALERT!

> The fast-track method does not work for bed-wetting. It is only for teaching children to use the potty during the day. Never chastise your child or expect him not to have accidents while sleeping. Youngsters have no control over them.

Each time your child wets or soils, have her practice telling the difference between wet and dry pants or clean and messy ones. Have her check her pants and tell you if they are wet or dry (or clean or soiled).

Then have her practice hurrying to the potty from the spot where you discovered the accident and back again five times. Each time she gets to the potty, she lowers her pants, sits briefly, raises her pants, and returns to where you discovered the accident. Even if you feel you are nagging, keep urging her to move quickly. The secret to avoiding accidents is going to the potty as soon as the urge hits and getting pants off fast.

 **ESSENTIAL**

> Always have your child help clean up accidents. Give her a sponge to clean up. Tell her to remove her wet clothes and put them in the laundry area. Have her wash herself and get into a clean change of clothing. Help her dress. Realistically, you will do most or all of the work.

If your child has a tantrum when forced to practice hurrying to the potty after an accident, let the tantrum run its course before you continue with the session. Pick up where she left off as soon as she calms down. When the practice session ends, encourage your child to participate in cleaning up and changing, but do not insist that she help.

While changing her, work on the self-affirmations by saying, "Mommy doesn't like wet pants. She wants you to urinate in the potty. Will you urinate in the potty?" so she will say or think, "I will urinate in the potty."

(E) ESSENTIAL

Show your child how to grasp the front of the waistband of his pants with both hands and bend his knees so he doesn't have to lean over so far while raising and lowering pants.

Slow Learners

Stop the lessons if exhaustion sets in. Continue to check your child's pants every fifteen minutes for the rest of the day, expressing pleasure and giving a reward of a drink when she is dry, or changing her if she is wet or soiled. She can't learn if she's tired, so do not make any other demands.

- Do not tell her to go to the potty. Just take her if it looks like she needs to use it.
- Do not have her practice running to the potty after accidents. Just change her.
- Describe everything she has done that was right.
- Keep her in underwear or training pants, but put on a diaper cover if she is still having accidents.

If you stop the sessions for a nap or at bedtime, pick up where you left off when she awakens. For the next two days, check your child's pants (instead of having her check them) immediately after she awakens in the morning, before and after naps, before snacks, before lunch and dinner, and before bedtime.

Special Considerations

If a child has diarrhea, a bladder infection, or an illness that prevents him from getting to the potty on time or at all, do not express displeasure or have him practice hurrying to the potty.

 **QUESTION?**

How long should I use salty foods or liquid rewards?
After the first twenty-four hours of training, do not offer rewards that increase urination. Try stickers or candy instead.

During and after training, put children over thirty months of age to bed in underwear and a waterproof diaper cover, and protect the bed with a waterproof sheet. That way, they can easily remove their clothes if they feel well enough to go to the potty or if they awaken at night and need to use it. Put younger children to bed in diapers. They will continue to need adult help going to the potty anyway.

Success!

Even after your child is using the potty regularly, continue to check his pants regularly for the rest of the training day, and offer sips and salty snack rewards so that he has lots of opportunities to go to the potty.

Children are trained when they go to the potty one time without prompting and can complete all the tasks without help. After accompanying your child to the bathroom a few times to offer praise and a drink or salty snack as rewards, confine yourself to an appreciative smile when she uses the potty. If you are rigorous about enforcing practices and helping children with self-affirmations, accidents usually decrease quickly. When your youngster goes two days without an accident, hold a big celebration! Help her relay the good news to other family members and friends. Bring out the cake and ice cream, and post a Potty Training Certificate on the refrigerator. While you're at it, give yourself a pat on the back, too.

CHAPTER 7

Potties-Without-Pressure Method

The pressure-free approach recommended by the American Academy of Pediatrics is ideal for busy families training older toddlers. It's the best way to stop power struggles before they start, and can help children who had bad experiences with other methods.

Changing Traditions

The potties-without-pressure method communicates a deep, abiding respect for children's bodies and honors each youngster's need to develop at his or her own rate. Parents do not introduce the potty until age two and one-half or three or even later, and must trust that their child possesses an inborn urge to grow up. They must have faith that their child's internal growth is continuing even when they cannot discern signs of progress. Parents confine themselves to teaching the readiness skills, letting their child watch them use the bathroom, and treating accidents with compassion, sympathy, and understanding. They never apply pressure.

As more and more parents use the potties-without-pressure method, the average age for potty training has increased dramatically. In the 1930s, parents started training infants around three months of age. In 1946, Dr. Spock suggested waiting until the baby was seven to nine months old. By the 1960s, 90 percent of children were not potty trained by age two.

In the early 1960s, author and pediatrician T. Berry Brazelton told parents to wait until their child was twenty-four to thirty months old before they started potty training. A study reported in the December 1989 issue of the *Journal of Family Practices* indicated that almost half of parents did not start potty training until after their child's second birthday. In 1999, Brazelton increased the age still further, suggesting that children would not be ready for training until after age three. His recommendations were officially adopted by the

American Academy of Pediatrics. ("Toilet Training Methods, Clinical Interventions, and Recommendations" by T. Berry Brazelton, Ann C. Stadtler, and Peter A. Gorski in *Pediatrics*, June 1999, volume 103, issue 6, p. 1359). Now, one-third of tots are still in diapers after their third birthday.

Ⓔ ALERT!

> Some older toddlers virtually train themselves overnight. Others have difficulty overcoming the entrenched habit of wetting and soiling, and require a long time to be fully potty trained. It is now common for four-year-olds to still be in diapers.

In just two generations, the knowledge that it is even possible to potty train younger children has been all but lost. Jan Faull, author of *Mommy I Have to Go Potty: A Parent's Guide to Toilet Training*, says, "pee and poop simply come out when the bladder is full" for younger children. She goes on to say, "How Grandma claims her children were completely trained at eighteen months or sooner is a mystery today." The answers can be found in the baby-track method! (See Chapter 4.)

Benefits and Drawbacks

By removing all pressure, the potty-without-pressure method affords children time to heal from previous negative potty training experiences. It can be ideal for working parents who cannot provide the consistency and time commitment younger toddlers require in order to learn. Since so many parents are using this pressure-free method, the stigma attached to wearing diapers in preschool has all but disappeared. Some children are still wearing them in kindergarten.

What It Means to You

The downside of this method is that parents have to continue to be involved with diapers and cope with accidents for a long time. Moreover, even this gentle approach can lead to struggles. Some children change their mind about the potty and stop using it, but refuse to go back to diapers. If they do not wear diapers, the lack of hygiene can be a real problem in the short-term, and the smell can endure in carpeting and furniture. And if they do go back to diapers, then rashes from urine and allergies from disposable diapers lead to a whole different set of problems.

Ⓔ **ALERT!**

An advantage to the potties-without-pressure method is that mastering the potty with so little help can boost children's confidence— and their parents' confidence in them. That can pave the way for greater autonomy down the road.

The recommended way to handle accidents actually does put some pressure on children, too. After all, if parents respond to every spilled glass of milk by saying, "It's okay, you're still young, you'll learn in time, better luck tomorrow," even the child who enjoys dumping milk and splashing in it would soon get the idea that it's not good to do that. Still, such gentle handling is less destructive than yelling, punishing, and shaming.

Other drawbacks of this method include the ongoing expense of diapers, which is tremendous. The idea of children "wearing their waste" is appalling to infant and baby trainers, as well as to members of the older generation. Continuing in diapers so long may be cruel if a child has chronic problems with diaper rash. Allergies to the chemicals used to manufacture disposable diapers and to sanitize cloth ones can be serious. Then there is the destructive environmental impact. Disposable diapers are the third biggest contributor to landfills.

Commitment and Self-Discipline— Yours

Although the lack of structure and direction are fine for independent, self-motivated, self-disciplined youngsters, other toddlers will need more concrete help, limits, and structure. In many ways, potty training is like learning to read. Some students learn with little help and only an occasional nudge from a teacher. Those who have trouble, or little or no interest in learning, need an active, involved adult. Patience to teach and encourage them and time are necessary if you plan to take this long-term approach to potty training.

Consider that pet owners can housebreak a puppy in short order by taking it outside shortly after a meal and using positive reinforcement to praise it for relieving itself outdoors. However, trying to train an older animal that has developed the habit of going in the house over a period of years makes housebreaking difficult indeed. After two years of constant wetting and soiling, diapers are a hard habit to break.

Still, the theory behind this extremely gentle approach is sound, and parents are wise to consider it.

How Long? How Soon?

There are no reliable statistics on how quickly older toddlers complete potty training when all decisions are left to them. Once they decide to tackle it, some children master it in a day or two. Many parents report that it took one to two months; most professionals say to expect about six months. One to two years is not unheard of. Sales of disposable diapers in extra large and jumbo sizes have ballooned as a result.

Research shows that lots of prior exposure to peers', siblings', and parents' toileting can promote early learning. Common sense suggests the following factors are influential, too.

Readiness—Of all the readiness skills (see Chapter 2), being able to sense urination and bowel movements in advance and get pants on and off quickly are paramount.

Motivation—The child sees a big benefit to using the potty and wants to learn.

Help seeking—The child wants help, asks for help, and is willing to follow suggestions.

Accident management—The parent remains calm and reassures the child that there is nothing to be upset about.

Desire to grow up—Children who want to be a "big kid" can proceed rapidly.

The usual pattern is for toddlers to complete bowel training before bladder training, though many finish both at the same time. However, complications due to pain from constipation or special fears about flushing tend to delay bowel training for about six months after bladder training is finished. Do not let your child become constipated or see his bowel movements be flushed away. Unlike other methods, in which children practice saying good-bye to their B.M.s, this method does not teach that flushing is the accepted practice. Even if your child does not seem upset when he sees his stool being flushed down the toilet, he might have a delayed reaction and become fearful later.

Big Kid Delights and Dilemmas

Some characteristics typical of three-year-olds can make them easier to potty train than younger children. Older toddlers tend to be less active than they were during the highly energetic two-year-old stage; they are also generally less oppositional and have less dramatic mood swings. They may more readily recognize physical sensations of fullness. They urinate less frequently because their bladders are larger, and they may be more able to delay the start of bowel movements. Certainly their more advanced language skills make it easier for you to communicate with them.

 ALERT!

The biggest problem with potty training older children is parental impatience. Adults can appreciate a younger child's small accomplishments but expect far more of older toddlers. After a couple of successes, parents' commitment to letting their child proceed at her own rate, as this method requires, may weaken. Be patient!

Some three-year-olds learn to use the potty with so little help, it is as if they taught themselves overnight. Unfortunately, there are no guarantees. Although an older child can understand more readily that waste comes from his body, learning to recognize the sensations of needing to eliminate in advance and learning how to relax the sphincter may still take some time. Many older children are more compliant than they would have been during the difficult two-year-old stage, but some are more oppositional. They may not think it is worth the trouble to leave enjoyable activities to use the potty. Despite older toddlers' sometimes noisy protests about having to be changed, diaper changes can be a comforting ritual they do not want to give up.

 FACT

> Severe conflicts about using the potty can cause children to block out their physical sensations so they can't tell when they need to use it. What may seem like purposeful wetting or soiling to you may really be accidents. Do not jump to the conclusion that your child is defying you.

Too many mentions of potties, questions about needing to use the potty, and warnings about impending accidents can make children feel that they are being pressured, which can trigger fears of failing, of disappointing their parents, or of making their parents angry. If parents can use extreme tact, they can occasionally mention that they will help if their child ever wants to learn to use the potty. They can invite her to sit on it to hear a story. They may express a desire for her to learn to use it someday. They can communicate pleasure when their child does express an interest in using it. Otherwise, parents should let their child's natural

THE EVERYTHING POTTY TRAINING BOOK

interest in learning determine when and how quickly she proceeds, and hold any dissatisfaction with the child's progress in check. If parents decide to change to an approach in which they make some demands, they need to communicate their intentions clearly. In the meantime, the challenge is to trust the process instead of trying to hurry it along.

Meet the Potty

Parents should be conscientious about teaching the readiness skills (see Chapter 2), but they should not make any concrete moves to introduce the potty until their child shows clear signs of wanting to learn. Signs include:

- Trying to use the potty
- Wanting to accompany other family members to the toilet
- Disliking wet diapers
- Persisting in removing diapers
- Being upset about diaper changes
- Going to a special place to wet and soil

When you think your child may be ready, let him help select a potty and choose underwear he likes. Explain that you are going to teach him to "Put your urine and B.M.s in the potty," but let him get to know the potty in his own way. Brazelton suggests that you not remove his clothes, as that could be a blow to his dignity or make him afraid.

(E) FACT

Some children like their potty from the start. Yours may well avoid it for a week or two—longer if she has had a bad prior experience, if your nervousness makes her leery of it, or if she has somehow concluded that the potty means trouble. Sit a stuffed animal on it to show her that it's safe.

Move Forward Slowly

Once your child can comfortably sit on the potty clothed, ask if she would like to try it without anything on her bottom. Ask permission before removing your child's diaper, and only remove it if she agrees. Then, if it looks as if she wants to, suggest she sit on her potty while you sit on the toilet, and explain that this is what mommies and daddies and big kids do. When parents demonstrate and verbalize the process of using the toilet, they capitalize on their youngster's natural inclination to mimic them.

Easing into the Next Steps

After a week of demonstrating, take your child to the bathroom to remove a soiled diaper and empty it into the toilet as your youngster watches. Explain that big people put their bowel movements in the toilet every day. Wait to flush until he has left the room.

On another day, ask permission to remove your child's diaper and put the potty nearby so he can use it if he wishes. If he agrees, ask if he would like to be reminded to use it about once an hour. If he says yes but doesn't respond when you remind him, that simply means he isn't ready. Drop the matter until he is. If he does use it, express mild pleasure but do not gush with delight. That takes the victory from the child. He might think he should keep using the potty to make you happy, which creates pressure.

Ⓔ ESSENTIAL

Do not let your child see you flush away his bowel movement. Even if a youngster seems unaffected at the time, the question about where that special part of him has gone can create anxieties and fears that later translate into constipation and potty refusals.

Going Without Diapers

You can lengthen the time your child spends without a diaper when you sense she might be really ready to use the potty. When an accident happens, tell her that it's okay. Remind her that someday she will be ready to use the potty like her parents, older siblings, relatives, and friends. Until then, however, put her back in diapers.

If she refuses to wear a diaper but won't use the potty either, assume she is embroiled in an internal battle. She doesn't want to go back to wetting and soiling herself, perhaps due to pressures from peers, but isn't ready to move forward and use the potty, either. Only she can resolve this dilemma. Do not try to push her one way or the other.

Ⓔ QUESTION?

My child wants to wear underpants but will not use the potty. What is going on?
She wants to be grown up, but isn't ready yet. The potty is a big step toward independence. Express confidence that your child will solve this hard problem in time.

Diaper Dilemma

Many children begin withholding stool as they struggle with the dilemma of not wanting to wear diapers like a baby but not being ready to join the world of big people and potties. If constipation becomes so severe that your child is in pain, it's time for you to step in and make the decision your youngster cannot bring himself to make. Put him in diapers so he can get comfortable having bowel movements again.

Disinterested Trainees

Some children happily use the potty for a time, and then lose interest. They would rather go back to diapers than having to use the potty and worry about accidents.

Others do not want to stop playing to use the potty and are unconcerned about accidents. If you feel angry because your youngster won't go to the potty when she needs to, consider what "won't" really means.

When a little one is holding herself and ignores suggestions that she go to the potty, is it because she doesn't want to leave the fun and games? Is she too immersed in what she is doing to think about what is happening to her physically, even though it is obvious to you? Does she think she can wait a while without losing control? Is she afraid of growing up and needs to be a baby a while longer? In truth, there is no way to know. If you are angry with her for having accidents, you may add to her emotional conflicts, which can slow down training even more.

Nighttime Continence

Even if your child uses the potty without fail during the day, she may still wet the bed. She may not awaken, or, if she does, may not feel like getting up. Carrying her to the potty at night is yet another form of pressure, according to Brazelton. Instead, when she stays dry four to six hours at a stretch during the day, try putting her to bed without a diaper to see if she is ready. If she's not, peer pressure may eventually work its wonders. When friends brag that they sleep in big-girl underwear, your child may be more motivated to try.

Many children cannot awaken until they mature sufficiently, and punishing a child for this problem is abusive. If a child does wake up when his bladder is full, placing the potty near the bed can motivate him to use it. You might offer to awaken him so he can use the potty before you go to bed. However, if you cannot wake him up, do not carry him there. Even if he uses it, he cannot claim the success as his own, Brazelton believes. Instead of pressuring him, suggest he wear a diaper until he is ready to use the potty at night.

Self-Defense for Parents

Americans from past generations, as well as parents in most other countries, are horrified to think of waiting so long to start potty training. One of the hardest things for parents to tolerate is criticism, and waiting until your child is three and proceeding so very slowly is apt to raise a few eyebrows.

 FACT

> Potty training young toddlers requires more consistent involvement than many working parents can provide. Since many four-year-olds are still in diapers, it is no longer the stigma it was in previous generations.

What can you say when a friend or relative suggests that something must be terribly wrong for your preschooler not to be potty trained? Sometimes, a humorous response can relieve tensions. "Well, Dad, you might say that she's a little stinker in more ways than one!" Or, "The experts say to wait until children give the signal. If he doesn't give it before he's eighteen, I'm going to get firm no matter what the doctors say." Or, "I thought you'd never offer! I'd be glad to let her spend days with you until you've trained her. I'll take her back when you're done."

Otherwise, honesty is the way to go. Consider these options:

- "Many modern experts recommend waiting until closer to age three, and I think they're right."
- "Between the weekend visits with her father and having to share me with the new baby, she's got enough to deal with. I don't want to add more stress to her life right now."
- "He's such a high-strung child, I've decided to wait so he'll have age and maturity on his side."
- "She's in day care during the week, so I have to use a method that doesn't require such intense parental and caregiver involvement. It takes a lot longer when there's less consistency."
- "Studies show it doesn't actually much matter when potty training starts. Children continue to have accidents until about age three anyway. There's not much point to hurrying."

As with many other aspects of parenting, potty training is a topic that always draws suggestions, opinions, and sometimes outright criticism from others. If you begin to doubt your decisions and methods, talk to your pediatrician and discuss your situation with friends and relatives.

CHAPTER 8
No More Accidents!

S trings of accidents can make you frantic, but fortunately, lots of solutions exist. Many tactics are available to help little worrywarts overcome potty fears and to convince independent tots to go to the potty instead of trying to hold it. The best tricks are the games that make the potty so much fun, your child won't be able to resist using it!

Accidents Are Just Accidents

Whether they are occasional or constant, accidents really are exactly that—accidents. If you think your child is just trying to upset you when her toilet terror reaches epic proportions or when she soils and wets anywhere and everywhere, then you should definitely get professional assistance to deal with such a difficult child. Otherwise, get professional assistance to stop taking your child's problems personally. As long as you think everything is about you, you won't be objective enough to figure out how to help her. When you encounter one potty disaster after another, mustering objectivity is difficult indeed. But before you schedule your first appointment with a therapist, review the following solutions to common potty training problems.

Toilet Terrors

Any kind of frightening potty experience can cause your child to have a training setback. That could be falling off of the potty or thinking that he might, falling in the toilet or imagining that he could, having a bad dream about a potty, being startled by a shout or slap while on the potty, or hearing a loud noise while thinking about the potty. Seeing Mr. Clean leap out of a toilet bowl in the TV commercial terrorizes many, many tots. When you're two years old, fantasy and reality blur all too easily, so it's easy to think that Jaws lives in the bowl and then believe it's true. After imagining some dire catastrophe, your child may refuse to go near the potty. If you press, he may become so hysterical that to insist would be to traumatize him further.

Toilets in public restrooms can be a real problem. The automatic kinds flush without warning. They are noisy, the water agitates violently, and the whoosh as the water is sucked away can be as loud as a vacuum cleaner, as if to warn him that he could be next. Carrying a portable potty that your child can use in the car may solve the problem until he's over a public restroom phobia. However, the rest of the world's toilets may still seem unpredictable and dangerous. If he decides the one at home is out to get him, you've got a real problem.

Ⓔ ALERT!

> Public toilets are noisy, the water agitates violently, and your toddler may think the whoosh as the water is sucked away is a warning that he could be next. Carry a portable potty in the car for a terrified tyke.

If your child's fears center around the toilet, see if he will use a potty chair. If he had a scare on his potty chair, try switching to a potty seat. Try dropping the word "potty" from your vocabulary. Maybe he needs to "visit Henrietta" and "sit on her lap," or see if Mrs. Tank is "hungry" or "needs a drink." Tie a ribbon or bow tie around its neck, affix a face with masking tape to the lid, and affix stickers inside the bowl above the water line. If that does not help, stop all practice sessions for a month to give your child time to forget. Do not even mention the potty.

A Tiger in the Tank

If your child has seen Mr. Clean leap from the bowl on TV or has heard the day care rumor that tigers, dinosaurs, or spiders live in toilet water, open the tank so he can see what's inside (too small for a tiger, that's for sure). Demonstrate how to flush from inside the tank by lifting the lever, so that he can watch how the water rushes in through a tiny hole (too small for a tiger, that's for sure) then stops when the tank is full. Show him where the water leaves the toilet bowl through the little pipe in back (too small for a tiger, that's for sure).

Ⓔ **QUESTION?**

No matter what I say, my child thinks that a monster lives in the toilet. What can I do?
Give him a magic wand or flashlight for protection. Explain that every time he waves the wand or shines the light around the toilet, the monster will weaken until it leaves or dies.

When logic does not work (though, sometimes it does), try standing your toddler on a stool next to the toilet so he is far enough away when he urinates to be out of harm's way. Girls can stand for both urine and bowel movements by putting one foot on each side of the toilet seat and bending their knees slightly so they do not make a mess. However, while you keep watch for tigers, hold your child tightly so she doesn't fall in. Since neither tigers nor Mr. Clean ever show their faces to adults, you could also sit on the toilet, spread your legs, and hold your child on your lap while he uses it.

(E) ESSENTIAL

If you are holding a fearful child while she's on the potty, do not even think about letting go until she lets you know it is okay. Then hold your arm in front of her so she can grab on if she needs to. If she loses trust in you, it will take even longer to overcome her fear.

Desensitization Training

You can help your child conquer her fear one step at a time if she is brave enough to try. Have her stand outside the open bathroom door so she can observe you while you use the toilet. Show her how to take deep breaths that will help her relax. Alert her before you flush. Once she can stand in the doorway without becoming upset, she can move one baby step closer the next time and watch again. She can then take another small step nearer each day until she is close enough to put her hand on yours as you flush. Don't press her to keep coming closer. Let her set the pace. When she is ready to start sitting on the potty, hold her tightly.

Praise every tiny little success for being "so brave." Point out other times during the day when she is also being brave, and ask her how she managed to contain her fear. This will build her awareness of her bravery and help her apply the same strategies she uses to conquer other fears to facing the potty.

Around Town

First your child drives you crazy because she's too scared to use public restrooms. Then she must see every toilet in every store and dawdles endlessly. Don't decide she couldn't possibly need to use the toilet yet again—nervousness about using a strange toilet can increase urinary frequency. Also, excitement or fear from being in such a novel situation may have made it hard for her to relax enough to void completely. Don't refuse to take her because she sat for three minutes in the last bathroom and never did use the toilet. If she is nervous about whether or not you will take her when she needs to go, the likelihood of an accident increases.

If you feel as though your outings are totally centered around the restrooms and your hands are tied, they probably are. Rest assured that this too shall pass. Be sure to take a change of clothes just in case she is so caught up in the excitement and nervousness at the prospect of having to use a strange toilet, she forgets to tell you when she needs to go.

Help Your Child Become Comfortable

To help lessen the likelihood that your child will feel afraid of public facilities, make it a point to use them often and have her accompany you *before* you begin potty training so she can start getting used to them. Let her tear off some toilet paper for you and wash her hands so she can participate. If she becomes afraid of using public facilities after you've started potty training her, carry a folding potty chair. For this to be a solution, she must have used it at home often enough to feel comfortable with it. If she is so fearful about strange bathrooms that she can't relax enough to use it, try having her use the portable potty in the car.

Ⓔ ALERT!

If your child is afraid to use strange potties, you can purchase a portable or fold-down potty in stores that carry potty seats and chairs, as well as through online shopping services. Folding seats designed to fit on a regular toilet may not be enough to alleviate your child's fears; look for a small stand-alone potty chair that folds down and have her use it at home until she gets comfortable with it.

When in the Restroom

When you're out with a curiosity seeker, allow extra time so she can check out all the toilets in town, but beware of industrial-strength models. The sudden violent swishing and noise may frighten her so much that she suddenly becomes afraid of public restrooms. Meanwhile, if the endless dawdling in every bathroom in every store is driving you crazy, remember that there should be something rewarding in all of this stressful potty training business. As far as many toddlers are concerned, the chance to explore the fascinating world of stalls, electric hand dryers, sinks, and faucets is about as good as it gets.

Teach your child to be respectful by not peeking under the stall to see what others are up to. Although toddlers are very curious, it's never too soon to teach good manners. Always keep your youngster within sight so she doesn't wander out and get lost. Give her something to do, such as holding your purse or the door, or engage her attention through conversation.

Toddler boys may have to be taken into the women's restroom if they don't have a dad in tow, and toddler girls will have to accompany their dads if no mom is available to take them. Don't entrust them to a stranger so they can use the correct facility.

Potty Fun

It is all too easy for potty training to become a stressful, grim affair for both parent and child. By introducing a little lightness and laughter, parents can end power struggles with their child and turn tears to smiles.

The Tickle Me Game

Some children just cannot comprehend that they should take themselves to the potty when they need to go, no matter how many times they've been told. Mommy has been directing all the diaper and potty stuff for so long, they just don't get it. Try a conversation like the following when you think your child will soon need to use the potty. Beware! All this silliness might cause enough giggling to result in an accident.

> *Parent:* Can you say "I'm going to go potty?"
> *Child:* Nods.
> *Parent:* Can you say "Me go potty by myself!"
> *Child:* "Me!"
> *Parent:* (Teasingly) "What? Are you going to the potty by yourself? Mama's gonna get you if you go to the potty."

Give her a tickle to get her started running, and continue the chase as long as she is heading toward the potty. Prompt by saying, "Are you going to the potty by yourself? I'm going to tickle you!" Stand at the bathroom door and wiggle your fingers. "If you urinate in the potty, I'm going to tickle you!" If she goes, say, "You went potty by yourself!" and tickle her. If she doesn't, tickle her anyway so she continues to love the game.

Whether she initiates the same chasing game two seconds later or you initiate it several hours later, change the ending and do not tickle her unless she uses the potty. Look disappointed and say, "No, you don't need the potty now." Then smile and add, "But when you use the potty, watch out! I will tickle you!"

Ⓔ FACT

> Bending, stooping, coughing, sneezing, and laughing can cause bladder accidents. The sudden rise in abdominal pressure creates higher pressure in the bladder than in the urethra. Toddlers can't control themselves. The problem will resolve itself when they are more physically mature.

Hopefully, she'll start initiating the "tickle me" game. To phase it out, start to chase her, but let her go by herself and call out, "If Tanya goes potty by herself, I'm going to tickle her! Did Tanya go potty yet?" When she calls, "I went potty," or comes to get you, run to check. If she used it, tickle her. Otherwise, say, "I don't get to tickle Tanya now. Maybe she'll use the potty later."

Nighttime Fun

Can't get your tyke to use the potty at night? She will have to get out of bed if she wants to see the glowing green toilet water, which can be detected only when the room is dark and a Poti Lite is hanging in the bowl. She may think this product is way cool, and be glad to leave her covers to see it! The unit hangs over the edge of the bowl, under the toilet seat so that the batteries hang outside and a flexible arm with a light extends into the bowl. Poti Lite can be purchased from ✍ *www.pottytrainingsolutions.com.*

Beat the Clock

See if your child can "beat the clock" by using the potty before the alarm sounds to signal the start of his next potty practice session. See if he can "beat the timer" by using the potty before his required three- or five-minute session of practicing sitting on the potty ends.

The problem with trying to beat the clock is that you must never set your child up to fail. Be aware that the excitement of this kind of race against time can cause the kind of tension that keeps youngsters from being able to relax enough to use the potty or causes them to lose control and have an accident.

Holding It!

Besides increasing the risk of accidents, holding in urine for long periods increases the risk of bladder infection. Carried to an extreme, containing urine can stretch the bladder to such a point that it becomes increasingly difficult for children to sense the contractions that signal their need to relieve themselves.

Timed Sits

If your child insists on "holding it" to the point of discomfort or accidents, set an alarm and take her to the potty every hour. Then set a timer and have her sit for a few minutes. Once she learns she must sit out the time whether or not she urinates, and you are equally pleased either way, she won't be hurrying and should be able to relax. When she has accidents, do not make a big deal out of them. Don't even have her clean them up. Just happily say, "There's your urine! I bet you feel better now."

 ALERT!

> A few minutes after your child uses the potty, check her pants for additional leakage of urine. If they are damp, repeat the after-potty pants checks each time she urinates. If leakage is a regular occurrence, notify your doctor.

Helping "Pee" and "Poop"

At certain ages, knowing that Mom wants her to "go" may be enough for a tot to decide she doesn't want to. The way out of this impasse is to help her understand that it is not a matter of what you want or what she wants. It's what "Pee" and "Poop" want. And what they want, of course, is to come out! Tell her so.

When your child is trying to prevent urination or the start of a bowel movement, explain that Pee and Poop are trying to get her attention so she will take them where they want to be—in the potty. Or tell her they are begging her to put them where they belong—in the potty. Or they are begging to go to their home—in the potty.

 FACT

> In the past, teaching children to "hold it" was thought to strengthen the sphincter muscles and help prevent wetting. Now this technique is viewed as potentially dangerous; it can create more serious problems than it can cure.

If your child is caught up in a struggle with herself, and holding in waste to the point of pain, explain that Pee or Poop need her help to get "home." What she needs to do is to sit on the potty and relax. It might help her to lie down and have her tummy rubbed. Suggest that drinking more water and eating more fruit and vegetables helps make Poop strong enough to get out. Although she would not make the culinary sacrifice for herself, she might be willing to do it for them.

The Circle of Life

Some children are comforted by learning about the circle of life: her B.M. is going to feed the trees and flowers so the plants will grow tall and beautiful. The birds and other animals eat the plants so they can grow big and strong and feed their babies.

From that kind of story, one toddler instantly over-came his reluctance about having bowel movements in the potty. His parents weren't quite sure what happened until they heard their chronically constipated son hap-pily explaining to his sister that the birds eat his "mar-bles." Thankfully, he was willing to do his part for the sake of the food chain.

Hiding It!

Toddlers are famous for being very possessive of their little lumps and piles. Whatever goes in the potty bowl or toilet is going to end up being flushed away, and that thought may be too terrible for a child to bear. Diapers, of course, are fine—no matter that your child has watched you scrape her gems into the toilet a million times. Who can fathom toddler logic? The simplest solution is not to flush or dispose of B.M.s until your child is out of the room.

Homemade Toys

However, your tot may decide her B.M.s aren't safe with you or anybody else. Anyway, they're *hers*—so what right has anyone else to take them away? She may retreat to a special place to have bowel moments and hide what she's up to. Then she may play with the great toys she made herself. No, you don't have a deranged child on your hands. This is normal. You can't let her do that, though. Putting wet or dirty fingers in her mouth could make her ill. Playing with her homemade Play Dough is a "no-no."

Getting Her into the Bathroom

Try to find a way to get her to do her business in the bathroom, even if she won't use the potty just now. The habit of standing or squatting to defecate may make sitting feel too awkward. If she sits on a potty seat, resting her feet on a stool so she can push while sitting may help. More likely, you will need to contrive a way for her to stand or squat during bowel movements. Provide a container that's small enough so she can stand over it, but big enough so aiming isn't a problem, or see if she will stand on paper towels to defecate.

If she must have a diaper, perhaps she can stand over it instead of putting it on so she can clean herself up afterward without help. By placing a stack of clean diapers next to the potty so she can simply take one when needed, there should be little more work for the parent than if she were fully trained. Teach her to fold soiled paper towels or the diaper carefully, and find a mutually agreeable place to store her precious packet, such as in a lidded diaper pail. If she needs privacy, stand outside the door so you can get in fast before the squishing and mashing begin.

If the Bathroom Isn't an Option Now

If she won't have bowel movements in the bathroom, show her how to lay out a towel to protect carpeting. Children should be taught to take the dirty diaper to the parent afterward, and to go to the bathroom to wipe their bottoms and wash their hands.

To help your child take the next step, try accompanying him to the bathroom and suggest that he first put the B.M. in the potty, promising to help him put it in a diaper afterward. (You can retrieve it with a serving ladle.) In that way, the child can become accustomed to using the potty and avoid having his B.M.s flushed away.

Ⓔ ALERT!

> Constipation can cause uncontrollable soiling. Softer feces leak around the hard mass and out of the body. Children cannot even feel the leakage, much less control it. For help with chronic soiling, see Chapter 10.

Accident Prevention

A power struggle does not mean that a little one is purposely trying to upset his parents. He's not consciously thinking, "I'll show Mom that she can't make me do this! I'll mess in my pants just to upset her!" Rather, the struggle is unconscious. Often children avoid all thoughts about the potty because it is a source of tension, parental anger, and personal defeat. When forced to sit on the potty, they don't know how to push to initiate bladder contractions to expel urine or how to relax the sphincter muscles to release stool. The minute another miserable potty session has ended and they put the whole matter out of their minds, they relax, and suddenly the urine and/or stool begins to flow. If they get in trouble for having another accident, they will be even more tense the next time they're taken to the potty. A vicious cycle develops, and the problem gets worse and worse.

 FACT

Do not restrict your child's fluid intake to cut down on daytime bladder accidents! The urinary urge intensifies when urine is more concentrated. Dehydration can cause constipation, which can create even bigger potty training problems.

The most effective solution for parents is to handle accidents calmly. Avoid reproaching your child but insist that he participate by changing his clothes and helping with cleanup. Until he is ready to comply, assign a time-out. That way, if you are convinced he is wetting and soiling "just to get you," he will soon lose his motivation to wet and soil if you don't get upset.

Tough Love

By age three children should be able to participate actively in cleaning up accidents, and there are compelling reasons for them to do so if they are destroying the carpet, generating tons of laundry, and making no effort to use the potty. It may be difficult not to be angry, but it is very important that you aren't. Your role is to teach, and there are merits to teaching them responsibility and how to help clean up.

Put a step stool by the washer and show your child how to put the dirty clothes in, push the button, and lower the lid. *Supervise carefully throughout this process. Store detergent and cleaning solvents where your child can't reach them, and add them to the laundry yourself. Do not ever let your child touch these poisons!* Afterward, have him help transfer the clothes to the dryer and push the button. Then have him put the clean clothes in the clothesbasket. He can work on his colors and shapes and sizes while learning to match socks (great for cognitive development) while you fold and separate. Then, help him put the clothes away in drawers he can reach so he can change himself with as little help as possible.

Ⓔ ALERT!

> Most parenting books say never to go back to diapers after putting a youngster in underpants, but why continue to beat your head against the wall, make your youngster miserable, and ruin the carpet? If he isn't ready, he just isn't ready. Maybe in a month he will be.

As you will soon discover, making your child help clean up is not abusive. On the contrary, he will probably be having so much fun that your desire to make him suffer as much as you are will be thwarted. Might he want to have another accident just so he can do all that great laundry stuff again? Probably. Find more laundry he can help with, but do not try to ruin his fun. Potty training will end in a month or a year—his laundry skills can make your life easier for the next two decades. Grin and bear it until the novelty wears off. When it does—and it will—he will be more motivated not to have accidents.

A String around the Finger

If you have tried everything you can think of and your child keeps forgetting to go to the potty, perhaps having her go about bare-bottomed can help her remember. Turn up the thermostat, tell her not to have an accident, and remind her to use the potty when it looks like she might need to. Like tying a string around a finger, the unusual sensation of having nothing on her bottom may help her remember. Girls can go naked under a dress; it might work for a boy to wear pants without underwear. If an accident happens, do not admonish or punish. Just start teaching your child how to help with cleanup.

When he is holding himself or looks like he needs to use the potty, ask if he wants to go to the potty or wants you to bring it to him. Sometimes offering a choice instead of telling toddlers what to do works better. If he declines both, tell him if he has an accident he will have to put away his toys until he helps clean up and changes his clothes. If he does have an accident, be true to your word!

If your child continues to have accidents, then it's time to teach some basic janitorial skills.

A Fast Solution

Read the method for practicing after accidents that is used in the fast-track method (see Chapter 6). Toddlers do not like these rigorous sessions, but they will definitely learn to get to the bathroom from any location in the house lickety-split.

Oops!

Cheer up your little overachiever by reassuring her that eventually she will remember to listen to her body when it announces that it is time for her urine to come out. Until then, accidents will happen. They are not the end of the world! Teach her to say, "Oops!" and learn that there is a way to fix every problem using the problem-solving strategies explained in Chapter 2.

Ⓔ ESSENTIAL

Teach your child to clean himself up by popping him into the tub after soiling accidents. That way, he learns to take responsibility for himself even if he's not having B.M.s in the potty. Engage in potty power struggles and you both lose. Remember that it takes two to have an argument!

Hold the Phone!

You have been telling your child to drop everything and call you so you can help him get to the potty on time. Now he does just that—every time you are on the phone or busy with the baby. Of course, when you race off to join him, he doesn't need to go. What can you do?

Swallow your irritation. Praise his "good intentions." Be true to the lesson you've been trying so hard to teach: When nature calls, everything else must stop until bladder and bowel have been attended to. Yes, it's hard being a parent. I know. I understand. But just do it.

Talking Cures

Most toddlers are not very verbal, and even if they are, they don't necessarily process information well by talking. However, some children do respond well to sit-down conversations. In the interest of moving potty training forward, it's certainly worth a try.

"Please!"

After age three, most youngsters develop the charming characteristic of being able to consider other people's perspectives and points of view. They may pick wildflower bouquets to give as presents, make pictures for parents' refrigerators, or cheer up friends who are feeling sad. In other words, they may be willing to do you a favor. Try saying, "Mommy doesn't like accidents. She doesn't like doing all that laundry. Please go to the potty, OK? That would be such a nice present for me!"

Of course, most toddlers know Mommy is supposed to take care of them; they are not supposed to have to take care of Mommy. Still, give it a shot. Just don't take a negative answer personally. It's not you, it's not them; it's the age.

Mom's Method

If you are limping along with intermittent accidents because your child is too busy to be bothered going to the potty, try having what my own mother called "the conversation." "In this house, we all use the potty. That includes you. Sonnas do not make these kinds of messes! Do you understand?" (Pause for effect.) "Do I need to remind you or will you just go?" Regardless of the answer, the next time baby brother looked like he needed to go, she would say, "Remember! In this house, we all use the potty. Sonnas do not make messes!" All of her "Sonnas do this" and "Sonnas don't do that" lines, used on important occasions, had already instilled a sense of family pride. The Conversation worked.

If it hadn't, she would have followed up with, "I guess you do need me to remind you since you can't remember that Sonnas do not wet their clothes. You may wear diapers when the baby sitter is here, but when you're with me, you will use the potty like the rest of the family." And then there would have been once-an-hour potty practices during which he either used it right away or sat for a minute or two to "think about why Sonnas use the potty instead of making messes." She was that kind of mom.

Parents as Counselors

When potty training seems hopelessly stalled, sometimes a brief counseling session can help. When your child is calm, find a private place for a quiet talk. Look your youngster in the eye and probe her negative feelings about the potty by saying, "You don't like to use the potty, do you?"

Then pause. Make it a long one. Maybe you will get a small shake of the head or nod. Maybe you will only see a tense expression, notice a quick subject change, or observe misbehavior meant to distract you. Do not be distracted. Instead, gently ask, "Honey, why don't you like to go to the potty?"

Ⓔ ALERT!

Just because your child does not respond when you ask questions and discuss potty training problems does not mean he's not listening and reacting internally. If you think your child never listens, you are undoubtedly wrong. Even if your words do not get through, your tone does.

Give your child time to think, but do not expect her to answer. She probably doesn't know, and she probably couldn't tell you even if she did. Hopefully, your question will encourage her to ponder the matter. Once she can identify the problem, she will have taken the first step to solving it.

Start to wind down your little session by providing reassurance: "Going to the potty may seem hard right now, but it will get easier for you in time." Your words may be incomprehensible, but your reassuring tone will communicate that you are on her side.

After your words (or tone) have had time to sink in, offer anything you can think of to help her:

- "Would you like to go back to diapers for a while?" (if she has not been wearing them)
- "Would it help if I told you when to go to the potty?" (if you have been letting her decide on her own)
- "Would it help if I gave you a surprise every time you used the potty?" (if she is not already receiving rewards)

Again, do not expect a response, but if you get one, treat her comments with deep respect. If you do not come up with any workable solutions or new things to try, conclude with, "If Mama can help you with the potty, let me know," and give her a reassuring hug and a kiss. If nothing else, this gesture should help to defuse power struggles.

Do not be surprised if a day or a week later your child suddenly reveals something that helps to explain at least part of the problem. She may say you should put diapers on her instead of on her little brother, which may mean she wishes she could be the baby again instead of a big girl who has to cope with potties. She may suddenly get upset because she wants her B.M. back after it has been flushed away, effectively letting you know that it bothers her when it disappears down the drain. She may suddenly dissolve into tears when you suggest she put aside her toys to use the bathroom, letting you know how she longs for the more carefree days when she didn't have to worry about accidents all the time. One boy finally revealed his toddler fear when he suddenly announced that the "spiders could bite me."

Comfort your child, sympathize with her plight, and reassure her that she is still your baby. Continue your usual potty routines and requirements, but try not to push her to grow up too fast. To the extent that it's possible, let her be what she is: a baby in oh-so-many ways.

CHAPTER 9
Health and Wellness

Your goal is to potty train your child, to be sure, but don't lose sight of the rest of the picture. Teaching good hygiene, providing a healthy diet, and offering lots of opportunities to exercise need to be high on your list of priorities, too. The habits your child develops during potty training may last for years—perhaps for a lifetime.

Hygiene

The habits children develop when learning to use the potty are likely to last a lifetime, so it is important to teach them to wash their hands and wipe properly, and to rinse the potty bowl and flush the toilet after each use. This is a good time to teach other points of etiquette, too, such as putting down the toilet seat and lid, wiping up splashes in the sink after hand washing, and straightening the towel before dashing off to play. Toddler boys need to be taught to pay attention when they urinate so they do not spray the floor and walls, and to clean up if they do. In general, youngsters need to learn to do their part to help maintain a room of the house they will use lots in the years to come.

Parents spend so much time dealing with their youngsters' waste, they can begin to take it for granted to the point that they forget to follow basic rules of hygiene. Similarly, parents find themselves spending so much time struggling with their youngsters' potty training problems and accidents, they do not want to make an issue of wiping and hand washing. Good hygiene really is important for your entire family's health. Be sure to give it the attention it deserves.

Hand Washing

Hand washing does more than keep toddlers' hands pretty and presentable; it protects them from disease. Failure to wash hands properly after using the toilet can cause illness—and it often does! Toddlers will inevitably get stool on their hands when they wipe themselves, as will caregivers when they change diapers and handle soiled laundry. Even traces too small to be seen contain germs. If a contaminated hand has a small cut, or if it touches the mouth or an eye, germs that cause illness enter the body. Be fastidious about washing your hands after you touch soiled diapers and laundry, and have your child come to you for a clean hands check after he has used the potty by himself.

Public restrooms are especially germ-filled, and studies show that about a third of people do not wash their hands at all, and another third don't do it correctly. Consequently, almost every surface is contaminated. Here are instructions on how to get the hand-washing job done right:

- Wet hands.
- Use liquid soap whenever possible; avoid wet bar soap.
- Rub hands vigorously to dislodge microscopic bacteria and viruses from ALL areas of the skin for fifteen to twenty-five seconds.
- Rinse thoroughly.
- Dry hands on a clean, dry towel.

Antibacterial soaps are all the rage these days, but scientists warn that their widespread use will result in resistant superbugs, as has happened from antibiotics and insecticides. Stick to plain soap.

Wiping

Children will not do a very good job of wiping themselves until kindergarten. Besides their lack of practice, their arms are just too short for their bodies. Teach your child to use several small pieces of toilet paper to clean himself, tossing each one as it becomes soiled. This is far more effective than toddlers' natural tendency to use a single big wad. Moistened towelettes can do an even better job, but children will need adult help to use them at first, too.

Starting at the vagina, girls should wipe forward with clean tissue after urinating so as not to get bacteria in the vagina or urethra. For the same reason, they should start just behind the vagina and wipe back along their buttocks after a bowel movement.

Keeping the Penis Clean

You need to make a special effort to keep the penis of an uncircumcised boy clean in order to reduce the risk of infection. The foreskin of an uncircumcised infant cannot be pulled back, but make it a habit to lift the foreskin gently as soon as it begins to loosen and wash the area carefully during each bath to prevent infection. Do this by gently wiping with a soft washcloth that has been dipped in warm water, and teach your tot how to do the same when he is old enough. When the foreskin is fully retractable so that it can be folded back over the penis like the cuff of a shirt sleeve over an arm, be sure your child returns it to its normal position after urinating or washing himself. If the foreskin is left folded, it can function like a rubber band. The resulting constriction can cause problems serious enough to require medical treatment.

Diaper Rash

Urine is very acidic and can wreak havoc with delicate baby skin. To help clear up diaper rash, change soiled diapers frequently. Try switching brands of disposables or use cloth diapers. Avoid wipes that contain alcohol, which is drying, and gently blot the skin instead of rubbing it.

 FACT

In the late 1800s to mid 1900s, parents dusted babies with plain white flour to keep them dry. Oldsters say to bake the flour at 300 degrees and stir occasionally until it is uniformly brown to keep it from becoming sticky and turning into dough. It can then be stored in a can near the changing area.

Protect against chafing by applying a cream containing zinc oxide. If there is irritation on the sides of the groin or around the waist, fold disposable diapers so the plastic liners face out and don't touch the skin. It can help a lot to have your child go bare-bottomed for ten minutes to be sure he is completely dry before putting on a clean diaper. If the rash worsens or persists for three days, the cause may be a yeast infection, which requires a prescription. See your pediatrician.

Bronchial irritants, including tolune, xylene, ethylbenzene, styrene, and isopropylbenzene, are among the chemicals typically found in disposable diapers, according to Rosalind C. Anderson, lead researcher for the diaper study summarized in a report entitled, "Acute Respiratory Effects of Diaper Emissions." The out-gassing of a straight-from-the-package diaper in a medium-sized room was high enough to produce asthma-like symptoms ("Acute Respiratory Effects of Diaper Emissions," by Rosalind Anderson and Julius Anderson. *Archives of Environmental Health*, 54, October 1999). If you see crystallized gel oozing on your child's bottom, that's part of the chemical brew used to enhance absorbency. Stick with cloth!

Bladder Health

It's not just an old wives' tale that cranberry juice promotes bladder health. Doctors recommend it, too. Drinking lots of water promotes frequent urination, which decreases the risk of bladder infections.

Bladder Infections

Bladder infections are more common in girls because the urethra is short, and in wiping after bowel movements they can get a bit of stool on the urethral opening. However, boys can and do get bladder infections, too. Bladder infections can increase the frequency of urination, and may also create an urgency so intense children can't get to the potty in time.

The typical symptom is blood in the urine, which turns it cloudy or pink. There may be a spot of blood on the toilet tissue after urination. Bladder infections can also cause loss of bladder control, frequent and/or painful urination, pain just above the pubic area or on the side, fever, and lethargy. They can be serious, so see your doctor fast.

Urinary Tract Infections

Toddler logic has it that what comes out should go in, so most boys will at some point use a squeeze bottle or squirt gun in the bath tub and inject some water into the place from which the urine flows. The result can be a urinary tract infection. Be sure to tell your child that he must never put water or anything else in his penis. Hope for the best but be prepared for the worst. Just as toddlers are driven to insert beans in their ears and peas into their nostrils, they are compelled to insert water into their penis.

 FACT

> Discharges from the penis are rare prior to puberty, but if you notice one, your child needs to be seen by a doctor. An infection brewing under the foreskin can produce enough pus to look like a discharge. That, too, requires prompt medical treatment.

Oil from the skin and small quantities of urine can easily become trapped under the foreskin of an uncircumcised penis if it is not cleaned properly, which can cause infection. Pus signals the presence of an infection that requires medical attention. In addition, associated swelling can prevent the flow of urine. Contact your doctor immediately.

Leakage

Additional leakage after urinating can signal a physical malformation correctable by surgery, so check your child's pants a minute or two after he uses the potty. Otherwise, you might think he had an accident an hour later when he didn't. Also, the stream of urine should be strong and steady. See your doctor if it tends to trickle out or often flows in erratic spurts, even when your child urinates a large quantity. Infants do this, but toddlers should not.

Ⓔ ALERT!

Frequent urination, few periods of being dry, and painful urination suggest the need for an immediate medical exam for a bladder infection even if urine is clear. So does frequent urination, even if it is because your child drinks large quantities. These can be warning signs of diabetes.

Food Allergies

Food allergies can have adverse bowel and bladder effects, from diarrhea to constipation to bladder irritation. The following are common culprits. Talk to your pediatrician about eliminating them from your child's diet for ten days to two weeks to see if the problem improves, only to recur when the food is eaten once again.

- Milk and dairy products. (Remember that cheese and butter contain milk!)
- Carbonated beverages.
- Artificial colors and sweeteners.
- Citric acid and vitamin C.
- Melons, especially watermelon and cantaloupe.
- Any other foods to which your child is known to be allergic.

Bowel Health

It doesn't matter how often your child has bowel movements. Some only defecate every other day, or even less. Some children have a natural tendency to be constipated. Eating a lot of highly processed (a.k.a. "junk") foods causes constipation, too, because they are absorbed into the system so completely, all that remains is a hard, heavy mass. The best cure is a diet rich in fruits, vegetables, and whole grains (especially bran, brown rice, whole wheat, and oats) to add lightweight bulk, and lots of water to soften it. Also, avoid foods that bind, such as bananas, chocolate, peanut butter, and cheese.

Fluid Intake

Toddlers need four to six cups of fluid daily under normal circumstances—more in hot weather or if they are ill with fever, vomiting, or diarrhea. Besides water (from the tap or bottled; plain or carbonated), good sources include soup, juice, and milk. However, milk provides only $2/3$ cup of fluid per cup; the rest is solids.

Pain and Pressure of Constipation

Serious problems with constipation or worse, with impaction, can complicate potty training. Small hard "marbles" don't usually cause a problem, but wide stool can be painful to pass and cause tears that take time to heal. Small drops of blood on underwear or toilet paper may signal that this has happened, as well as rectal itchiness, which occurs as the tears start to heal. Gently wash the anus with soap and water after each bowel movement, and have your youngster soak in a warm bath to ease the pain. Put a dab of petroleum jelly on your finger and insert it into your child's rectum to help protect the sore area.

The added pressure on the bladder from a lot of hard stool can give children less time to get to the potty, so they have more wetting accidents. Since a full bowel leaves less room for the bladder, it can't hold as much urine, so urination is more frequent. The pain of constipation can also blur the sensation of needing to urinate, so children have difficulty realizing when they need to go to the potty. It can hurt to urinate, too. It can cause encopresis, too (see Chapter 10).

ⓔ ESSENTIAL

Improper diet and insufficient exercise are the leading causes of constipation. Give your child snacks of veggies and fruits instead of crackers and candy. Turn off the TV and clear an area in the house for lots of vigorous play. These measures will enhance your child's ability to sit still on the potty, too.

Psychological Constipation

Emotional factors can undermine children's ability to relax the anal sphincter at will so it will release stool, resulting in psychological constipation. Sitting on a cold toilet seat, potentially being splashed by cold water (if a potty seat is used), watching part of oneself being discarded and sucked down a noisy drain, and losing the special time one-on-one time while a beloved parent wipes and cleans and rubs them with sweet-smelling creams and lotions—is this what being a big boy is all about? Stress during potty training can cause constipation. Add to that a diet rich in junk food and low in fiber, and it's no wonder toddlers become constipated.

Shaping up your child's diet might help. Otherwise, doses of mineral oil will make it impossible for your youngster to hold back a bowel movement while softening the stool enough so passing it doesn't hurt. But is dosing a youngster with mineral oil to pry out feces an invasion of bodily integrity? Consult your conscience as well as your pediatrician to decide. Inquire about the possible need for vitamin supplements.

Remember that it's one thing to administer laxatives, stool softeners, and enemas to youngsters who are suffering from constipation or impaction because a pediatrician prescribed them. It's quite another to dose children with laxatives instead of straightening out their diet. And using laxatives to ensure your child has bowel movements at particular times so you can get her on the potty during potty training should be considered some sort of abuse. Don't do it!

Ⓔ FACT

Potty training is actually potty teaching: "to discipline" means "to teach," and "a disciple" is "a pupil." This is your chance to learn that disciplining your child means teaching her. As you experience the power of positive teaching methods to help her learn quickly and create a loving relationship, you will learn the most powerful lesson of all: how to be a really wonderful parent.

Diarrhea

Children don't have much if any bowel control during even minor bouts of diarrhea. Put them back in diapers and forget potty training until they're over it. Avoid foods that have a laxative effect, especially raw fruits and vegetables and concentrated fruit juices.

The main risk of diarrhea is dehydration, which is dangerous if it goes on for very long, and can become dangerous very quickly if combined with vomiting and high fever. Taken to an extreme, it is fatal. Lost minerals such as chloride, sodium, and potassium must be replaced quickly. Give your child Gatorade or another electrolyte solution and contact your doctor if you note any signs that serious trouble is brewing: cracked lips, decreased urination, darker or deeper yellow color of urine, urine that appears to have crystals, a sunken soft spot on the head of a young toddler, listlessness, increased pulse.

Head straight for the emergency room and try to get her to drink a Gatorade type preparation en route if there are no tears when crying, the cry is weak, breathing is weak, the surface of the tongue is dry, the skin feels cool, the skin of the hands and feet is mottled, the eyes appear sunken, there has been no urination for four hours, the skin is less wrinkled and elastic, or if after pinching a finger or toe, skin color takes more than a second to return to normal (this test assumes the child has been in a warm room).

Penis Health

At birth the foreskin is fully attached to the penis. It gradually begins to loosen, and by age one the glans at tip of the penis itself should be visible. Most boys' foreskin is fully retractable by age four or five, although for a significant percentage this doesn't occur until much later. At that point the foreskin can be folded back over the penis so that it is fully exposed for proper cleaning. The foreskin must never be left folded. That is dangerous and requires an immediate doctor's visit if the penis swells to the point that the foreskin cannot be readily unfolded. Often cold compresses and medications to reduce the swelling are sufficient to return it to normal, but sometimes minor surgery is required to relieve the constriction.

Because uncircumcised penises require special care, parents commonly opt to have the foreskin surgically removed. Although this custom is on the wane, many people still claim there are only benefits to circumcising a child. In fact, a circumcised penis is easier to clean, which reduces the risk of infection. However, infants do feel the pain from the surgery. Moreover, the widespread belief that circumcision does not impact adult sexual functioning is false. The exposed tip loses a good deal of sensitivity.

Chapter 10
Special Problems

Has your child overcome many potty training hurdles but continues to wet the bed at night? Have chronic wetting or soiling accidents? Have problems with constipation or urination? If you think your child might have a medical problem, turn to your child's pediatrician for help.

Getting Help

If you're having problems with potty training, the first person to turn to for help is your child's pediatrician. Doctors with this specialty work with potty training problems day in and day out, and are extremely knowledgeable about the subject. In addition to their technical knowledge, pediatricians have dealt with hundreds or even thousands of youngsters, which gives them a substantial basis for comparison. Although it may be true that no one knows your child as well as you do, professionals are in a better position to be objective about your child's capabilities.

When talking to your child's doctor, be honest and forthcoming when sharing your potty training problems, as well as the steps you have taken to correct them—even if it means admitting things that you have said and done that you think were wrong. To hold back is to do your child and yourself a disservice. The truth is that no parent feels very confident about how they have handled all of the difficult problems that can arise during potty training, and if they do, they probably shouldn't!

If you don't feel comfortable confiding in your child's pediatrician, schedule some interviews and find a different doctor. Since there's nothing like hearing other parents' struggles to give you a new perspective on your own, consider joining a parenting group, too.

Staying Dry at Night

If children have bladder control during the day, they are likely to have it at night, too, which means that it's time to stop using diapers. Sleepy children cannot use the potty easily if they are in diapers, so wearing diapers to bed encourages wetting and soiling. Instead, use a rubber pad to protect the bed and put waterproof pants over pull-ups so your child can get them off to use the potty at night. Or, try putting a PODS in his regular underwear (see Chapter 3).

Although full-blown fears of the dark do not typically develop until after age three, precocious children may feel uneasy at night at younger ages. Move the potty chair into the bedroom or light the way to the bathroom with nightlights. The prospect of company can be an incentive for a little one to get out of bed at night, so encourage your child to awaken you so you can take him to the potty.

Do not let her drink a lot of liquids after dinner, and take her to the potty before she goes to bed. Take her before you go to bed, too, and set an alarm to awaken yourself so you can take her to the bathroom once or twice a night. That may help her develop the habit of waking up to use the potty once she is mature enough to wake herself.

Ⓔ ESSENTIAL

To avoid urinary accidents, be sure your child avoids caffeine like the plague. Read the labels on coffees, teas, and sodas carefully. Avoid noncaffeinated carbonated beverages, too.

In the meantime, be patient. Most children have been conditioned to urinate in bed for several years. Disposable diapers reduce the discomfort of wetting to the point that many youngsters don't awaken even after they have had an accident, or they don't awaken because they simply sleep too deeply.

The Bedwetting Blues

There are three main causes of bedwetting: motivational, physical, and "deep sleep." It can be hard to tell whether bedwetting stems from the I-don't-feel-like-getting-out-of-bed-to-use-the-potty-at-night syndrome as most parents tend to think at first.

Physical Causes

Physical problems ranging from small bladder size to a bladder infection can cause incontinence. Many can be easily corrected. Sleep apnea can prevent children from awakening so they can use the potty; the brain never receives the bladder's signal that it is full. Eventually the sphincter gives way, causing an accident. If apnea is due to problems with the adenoids and tonsils, it can be easily treated. Apnea is sometimes difficult to diagnose because obvious symptoms may only be present at night, so children can appear healthy when examined by a doctor. Bedwetting also can infrequently be the result of bladder infection, a hormone deficiency, petit mal seizures, diabetes, a small bladder, a physical abnormality or malformation, or a central nervous system disorder.

Deep Sleep

Physical problems are thought to affect less than three percent of children. The usual problem which causes millions of youngsters to wet the bed is that they sleep so deeply, they simply don't awaken so they can use the potty. They may have some dry nights, but if they can't manage to go a full month without wetting the bed, the diagnosis may turn out to be "primary enuresis." What keeps them from awakening isn't understood.

 FACT

Only 45 percent of girls and 35 percent of boys stay dry at night before age three, according to an article in *Pediatrics*. As many as 25 percent of children have relapses after they have been dry at night for six months or longer (*The Gale Encyclopedia of Childhood and Adolescence.* Jerome Kagan, Executive Editor; Susan B. Gall, Managing Editor. Detroit, Mich.: Gale Research, 1998).

Boys, who are known to mature more slowly than girls, are more likely to be bedwetters, and since 15 percent of bedwetters spontaneously outgrow the problem every year, physical maturity is thought to be a factor. Most bedwetters have relatives who had the same problem as children, so heredity is thought to play a role.

Children who stay dry every night for a month and then start wetting the bed again probably have "secondary enuresis." The usual causes are fatigue, stress, and depression, all of which cause children to sleep more soundly than usual. Like youngsters suffering from primary enuresis, they are unable to wake up. The problem can be expected to disappear as soon as the child is back on an even keel.

Bedwetting Cures

Beware of the pediatrician who suggests your child just "isn't trying" without first doing a full medical exam (to rule out organic problems), a psychological exam (to rule out changes in the child's life that could cause increased exhaustion or stress), and a thorough family history (to investigate the possibility of an inherited problem). Since secondary enuresis is caused by stress and depression, and since punishing children causes them to feel stressed and become depressed, it is imperative that you react to bedwetting gently and with kindness. Otherwise, you'll make the situation worse rather than better.

Try-for-Dry

If your child wets the bed because of a chronic inability to awaken, be careful of the many outrageously overpriced treatment programs from companies with questionable reputations that prey on desperate parents. One safe one is Try-for-Dry. It offers a free self-guided diagnosis and treatment program at ✍ *www.tryfordry.com* so that parents need only purchase the materials they need. Or contact the Try for Dry patient liaison at Children's Memorial Hospital of Chicago Department of Urology at (773) 880-4428 or email *info@tryfordry.com*.

Restricting Fluids

The common practice of restricting fluids in the evening is a controversial cure which probably won't help. Do eliminate liquids that irritate the bladder and increase the frequency of urination (such as caffeine), check for food allergies (see Chapter 9), and avoid lots of fluids late in the evening, but know that normal fluid intake does not cause bedwetting. Good hydration is necessary for your child's health. When children are dehydrated their urine is more concentrated, which increases urinary urgency. It's the inability to awaken that drives enuresis.

Determine Patterns

If the problem is your child's inability to awaken so he can use the potty, treatments aren't much help before age five or six. Some parents claim to have re-set brain wave patterns during sleep by managing to bring their children to a state of complete wakefulness several times each night when they were very young.

Bedwetting specialists recommend that parents of toddlers try to determine the time at which the accidents typically occur by conducting frequent diaper checks or outfitting children with a moisture-sensitive unit that activates an alarm when urination begins. When the unit's electrical pad is moistened, a circuit closes and rings a bell or sounds a buzzer. In the past, these were very pricey items; now they are readily available through outlets that specialize in potty training products.

(E) ALERT!

Don't try to cure your child's bedwetting by severely cutting back on fluids. Doing so makes the urine more concentrated, so your child's urge to urinate will be more intense. When she does have to go potty, she'll have a hard time getting there fast enough.

Keep track of wetting incidents for a week. Once you've established your child's patterns, awaken him ten to twenty minutes before he is likely to wet the bed and take him to the bathroom to see if he can use it. Even if he never fully awakens, you may be able to avoid some accidents. Moreover, if you can consistently head them off for several months, you may be able to cure the problem by conditioning him. Exactly how this conditioning works is not understood. Rather than learning to get up at night, most children who have been successfully conditioned simply sleep through the night and stay dry without ever using the potty. If wetting starts up again after they have been conditioned, parents may need to take them to the potty every night for a few days to provide their brain with a "tune-up."

Medications

Some medications can be helpful to bedwetters, though they are not typically used with children younger than age five or six.

- Imipramine (also known as Tofranil) is the most commonly prescribed medication for bedwetting. Although this tricyclic antidepressant can be helpful to older children, the many difficult side effects make its advisability questionable. They include mood changes, nightmares, constipation, dry mouth, cardiac arrhythmia, drowsiness, restless legs syndrome, hypotension, confusion, tremor, dizziness, jaw cramps, and more!
- Oxybutynin chloride is a bladder antispasmodic which has proved helpful to many bedwetters. However, Stanford University researchers Barbara R. Sommer, William Kennedy, and Ruth O'Hara, Ph.D., note that adults who use this medication begin to show impaired memory and intellectual functioning. While the effects on children have not been studied and remain unknown, these doctors believe it is likely to have the same troubling effects. Known side effects include irritability, facial flushing, irritability, and heat exhaustion during hot months.

- DDAVP or Desmopressin is the synthetic version of a hormone the body normally produces at night. It recycles water from urine and moves it back into the bloodstream, thereby decreasing the volume. That's why even though most people urinate every few hours during the day, they are able to sleep through the night without having to get up to use the bathroom. Although DDAVP is a common treatment for chronic bedwetting, it too has difficult side effects, including nosebleeds, flushing, hypertension, and hypotension. In addition, it can interact with a wide range of medications. Bedwetting typically resumes as soon as the medication is discontinued. Still, it is a boon to older children, who may be able to use it as needed so they can attend sleepovers and summer camp.

Bedwetting Management

Be kind to your bedwetter! In an effort to protect themselves from continuing blows to their self-esteem, some youngsters adopt an I-could-care-less attitude. Parents may mistakenly conclude that they are not motivated to solve the problem or worse—are purposely wetting the bed—and react by becoming increasingly punitive. Since stress and depression cause secondary enuresis, parental negativity, shaming, and harsh punishments can cause what might have been a passing problem to become entrenched.

Instead, provide sympathy and reassurance that

your child is still too young to awaken at night. Limit fluid intake after dinner without being overly restrictive so that your youngster remains well hydrated. Have him use the potty before bed, and take him before you turn in for the night. If that does not work, track his wetting patterns and carry him to the potty to try to head them off as per the instructions explained previously. Put out clean pajamas if he is old enough to change into them by himself, and spread a sleeping bag on the floor so he can crawl into a clean, dry bed without awakening you.

Ⓔ QUESTION?

What prevents the smell of old urine from reappearing in bed linens?
Chlorine bleach and regular laundry detergents don't kill the bacterial spores that grow in urine, so the odor will reappear after linens and clothes have been washed. Try first soaking them in an enzyme bleach or borax solution.

Look for ways to lighten your workload. Use a vinyl sheet to protect the mattress and a waterproof cover over a diaper or pull-ups to contain the wetness. Even preschoolers can help remove soiled linen, and load the washing machine (as long as they do not touch detergents and cleaning solvents!). Do not assign these tasks as a consequence or punishment! Enlisting children's help in the cleanup process gives them something positive to do about the problem and helps to relieve their guilt.

Boy/Girl Issues

Children like to experiment, and it is common to try to use the bathroom like the parent or older siblings of the opposite sex. Toddlers are barely beginning to comprehend the differences between boys and girls. Since they learn by doing, they need to go through the motions. Watching and talking are not enough to satisfy their curiosity.

- Little boys may want to use toilet paper after they urinate because Mom does. Toilet paper is fun to use and doesn't hurt anything, so let them.
- Little boys may want to stand up to urinate because Dad does. Even though their aim is poor, let them stand and show them how to push their penis down so they can give it a try. Either sitting or standing is perfectly acceptable for a tyke, though sitting is far less messy.
- Some little girls want to stand up to urinate because Dad does. Lift your daughter so that she is standing up with one foot on either side of the toilet seat, keeping your hands on her waist so she doesn't fall. Encourage her to bend her knees slightly so she doesn't make a mess.
- Some children like to sit facing the tank, and it

becomes a habit. There is nothing wrong with sitting backwards! Indulge your child.

End messy experiments by saying, "Mommies and little girls/boys sit. Big boys and daddies stand up to urinate and sit to have a B.M." However, until children's curiosity is satisfied, they will probably conduct their experiments in secret, which can be far messier. It is safer—and neater—to guide them.

Playing in Feces

Touching. Smearing. Playing. Seeing youngsters handle feces can be very disgusting to adults, who have been conditioned to be repelled by the odor and realize all too well the health hazards. Little ones don't yet share their views. As far as they're concerned, stool is wonderful stuff for molding and rolling and pounding.

Rather than being harsh or even attempting to communicate disgust, most experts suggest a simple, "No, we don't play with that," followed by careful washing for a minimum of twenty seconds with soap and warm water. It's important to clean under their fingernails, too, before drying their hands thoroughly.

Offer Other Gooey Goods

Increasing opportunities to play in other gooey goods such as mud and wet sand may lessen the urge to play with bodily wastes. Otherwise, sanitized versions such as Silly Putty, modeling clay, Play Dough, and finger-paints may help.

Allowing Children to Explore

Some experts point out that even a simple "No" is enough to spark determined persistence among toddlers going through the oppositional two-year-old stage. Since children are infamous for sneaking into the bathroom or hiding behind a sofa to explore their bodily products, and since forbidding activities serves to increase some youngsters' interest in them, these experts say it's better to let them satisfy their curiosity in the bathroom with an adult standing by to supervise. That way, the parent can be sure none of the stool makes its way into the mouth or an eye (definitely dangerous!) and can carefully clean them up afterward. This more lenient approach makes it less likely that youngsters will feel ashamed about having bowel movements.

(E) ESSENTIAL

Although some experts recommend letting children play with stool to satisfy their curiosity and move past it, this is risky. Bacteria can enter their skin through a sore too small to see. If you do allow your child to handle his waste, supervise carefully to be sure he doesn't get it in his mouth, and carefully wash him afterward.

Feelings of embarrassment or shame can lead children to withhold stool, which causes problems with constipation or even encopresis (see below). If allowed to explore, hopefully they'll quickly satisfy their curiosity and move on to other, less noxious projects. It should be noted, however, that bacteria can enter the system through any skin opening, including small cuts and scrapes on the hands. Parents really do need to weigh the pros and cons before deciding how to handle this situation.

Encopresis

Why do so many children learn to have bowel movements in their potty chair, only to regress when using the potty seat on a toilet? Why do some children who have been successfully potty trained suddenly start having bowel movements anywhere *but* the toilet? Why do some children soil their clothes endlessly?

A Vicious Cycle

In the absence of a medical problem, a particular chain of events can lead to a lot of resistance or even full-blown encopresis—chronic soiling. It often begins when a child is slightly constipated, so the stool is a bit harder than normal. When it lands in the toilet bowl, the cold water splashes, hitting his bottom. The combination of surprise and discomfort makes the youngster nervous, even a bit afraid, of having a B.M. in the toilet again. He becomes tense and starts trying to hold in bowel movements to the point that he becomes constipated. When he does manage to have another bowel movement, the hard stools are painful to pass and produce more splashing.

A vicious cycle develops if a child is reluctant to pass stool for any reason, and he can become increasingly constipated. Bowel movements become increasingly hard and painful, which further adds to the child's reluctance to pass them. The situation can escalate to the point that a mass too large and hard to pass through the rectum forms in the bowel. Liquid which can't be absorbed leaks around the mass and exits. The child cannot inhibit the flow. Chronic, involuntarily soiling occurs.

 FACT

> Even slight constipation stemming from any cause can turn into a full-blown case of encopresis. Often, parents have no idea what is happening. The child has no control and can't feel when he is soiling.

Treatment for Encopresis

To break the cycle, the first step is to overcome problems with constipation. If that isn't enough, check with your child's pediatrician about mineral oil or a stool softener that will, once it takes effect, prevent him from holding it in. The oil may take a few days to work, so if your toddler is extremely constipated, a glycerin suppository or enema may help him get started. Since mineral oil can interfere with vitamin absorption, administer it several hours after a meal or before bedtime. Mixing the mineral oil in juice can make it more palatable.

A typical starting dose of mineral oil is 1 teaspoon per ten pounds of body weight given at night, or divided into $1/2$ teaspoon at morning and at night. The daily dose can be increased to three teaspoons. If you give too much, it may leak out, leaving stains on your child's underwear. Because mineral oil increases the risk of vitamin depletion, consult your pediatrician to see if your child needs a multivitamin. If the bowel movements become too frequent or watery, the dosage should immediately be reduced.

Create Positive Associations

Because children in this situation have come to associate the potty with physical pain and discomfort, breaking the negative associations and creating new, more positive ones may take a while and require a lot of help. Once the mineral oil takes effect and the child has been having regular soft bowel movements for ten days, rectal soreness should be completely healed. At that point, it is time to help your child have bowel movements while sitting on the potty.

For starters, have your child sit on the toilet for five minutes every day at the time he usually has a B.M., wearing pull-ups to ensure he is not splashed. If his resistance is too strong to be overcome by reassurance and pep talks alone, offers of toys and special privileges may be necessary. Provide a reward for just sitting on the toilet. Have him engage in a quiet activity he enjoys, such as reading a book to him, playing with an Etch-A-Sketch, or reciting nursery rhymes.

Ⓔ ALERT!

Protect your encopretic child from getting splashed by cold water when having a B.M., as this can lead him to withhold stool again. Have him stick to a potty chair until he is over his fears of having B.M.s, then reintroduce him to the toilet.

Once reluctance about sitting on the toilet has been overcome (meaning he sat without a struggle for three days in a row for five minutes each time), and he is completely healed, up the ante by making rewards contingent on having a bowel movement while sitting on it, but leave his pull-ups on to prevent splashing. If he doesn't go during his daily five-minute regime of sitting on the toilet, provide verbal praise and tell him he can still earn the reward if he has a B.M. in the toilet later. Instruct him to tell you when he needs to use it.

After a week of regular bowel movements while sitting on the toilet, your child should be ready to try having a bowel movement into the toilet. Remove his pants. Continue to set a timer to ensure he sits for five minutes, but only provide a reward after he actually uses the toilet, which might be later in the day.

Psychological Issues

Parents can begin reducing the mineral oil at any time the stools have remained consistently soft. Eliminate it gradually over a two-week period. Don't be surprised if the problem flares up again. Do what you can to protect your child from further psychological harm. Many people, including some psychologists, believe this kind of chronic soiling is a very disturbed way to express repressed anger. Adults' aversion to chronic soiling and lack of familiarity with the causes and cures has contributed to the belief even among many professionals that encopresis is a severe mental or behavioral disorder. Indeed, the stigma is so intense and peers' reactions may be so unfavorable, sufferers can quickly develop serious psychological problems. Children with this medical problem are often depressed, socially maladjusted, and have behavior disorders. But that is the result of this problem, not the cause.

If caught early and treated with compassion, there is nothing to suggest encopretic children have more serious adjustment problems than a child who has never experienced this problem.

Time Out!

Employees need coffee and lunch breaks. People need vacations. Football players need time-outs. Don't let potty training take over your life! Be sure to talk to your child about other things. Read books on other subjects. Praise your child for other accomplishments.

Being too preoccupied with the state of your child's bowel and bladder is likely to create the kind of stress that leads to burn-out and rebellion, depression and stress, and a wide range of physical, emotional, and psychosomatic problems. Unending concentration on potties conveys that success in this area is all that matters—and that's just not true! Your child's worth as a person is the same whether or not he is accident-free today or tomorrow or in the next six months. By high school graduation everyone manages!

If potty training is too intense for too long, you can lose your patience and objectivity. Although the diaper years can seem long indeed, someday you'll look back at this stage and be able to smile about it. You may not believe it now, but it's true. So why not start now?

APPENDIX A

Frequently Asked Questions

After reading *The Everything® Potty Training Book,* you will have a lot of information to process. If you have a specific question, read on for answers to a baker's dozen of parents' most common questions.

Q: What is the best age to begin potty training my daughter?

• • •

A: That depends on whom you ask—and when. In 1928, psychologist John Watson urged parents to hold a little pot under their infants starting in the first weeks of life. Until then, parents typically began training at age two to three months. In 1945, author and pediatrician Benjamin Spock recommended parents wait until babies would sit up by themselves. In 1961, author and pediatrician T. Berry Brazelton recommended waiting until the toddler years. Later he suggested it might be better to wait until around age three. Most cultures in the world still begin at two to three months of age.

It is usually best to begin potty training before children are mobile, assuming a stay-at-home parent can work with them regularly. After that time, psychological factors become important. In general, it is best to avoid the "overly active ones" and "terrible twos," but if your daughter can sit still as required (difficult for many one-year-olds), can cooperate (difficult for many two-year-olds), or is exceptionally motivated, toddler training may be fine. Otherwise, it may be best to wait until close to age three, or even later.

Q: My son would rather have an accident than go to the potty when I tell him to, and if I insist, he throws a tantrum. What can I do?

● ● ●

A: You can't make your son take off his pants or sit, much less use the potty, but you can hold a "potty practice" every hour or two, or whenever you think he needs to use it. Stay with him in the bathroom for no more than five minutes. Don't talk except to remind him that he's supposed to practice sitting on the potty. Sit on the toilet and read a book (or pretend to) to show him what he's supposed to do.

The key is not to become involved in a power struggle. If he decides to use the potty, don't praise or reward him. Just say, "You used the potty. You can go play." If he doesn't, say, "Your practice is over. You can go play." If he wets himself during potty practice, just say, "You wet your pants. I'll change you, then you can play," when his five-minute practice ends. Once he understands how potty practice works, announce when it's almost time, and tell him that if he can use the potty before the practice starts he will get a reward. Otherwise, have the session as planned.

Q: My daughter sits on the potty and we sing, read books, listen to music—whatever—but nothing happens until I put her diaper back on. Then not only does she go almost immediately, but she also gets very upset about it.

• • •

A: Contrary to what you might think, your daughter is trying to cooperate. The problem is she is trying too hard. As long as she is nervous, her muscles are tense, and that includes her sphincters. Without realizing what she is doing, she is holding in her urine and stool. When you put her back in a diaper she finally relaxes. Her sphincters relax, too, so she begins passing waste.

Eliminate the fun and games and see if sitting quietly helps. If not, have her go without a diaper for four or five hours every day. Try to keep her in the kitchen or another room that won't be destroyed by accidents. Keep the potty nearby, but tell her not to worry about using it or having an accident. She needs pressure-free time to focus on her physical sensations so she can notice how her muscles move when she passes waste. When she figures out how her body works, she'll be able to figure out how to tense and relax the proper muscles willfully.

Q: My son was almost potty trained, but now he won't have a B.M. in the toilet. He has a small B.M. in his pants several times a day. Sometimes he wets, too. He doesn't seem to notice or even care. I'm at a loss.

• • •

A: This sounds like a classic case of encopresis. When children become constipated, a mass of stool too hard to pass stays in the bowel. Softer feces make their way around the mass and leak toward the rectum. When the anal sphincter opens to release them, the urinary sphincter opens, too, so children end up wetting when they soil.

Even if your child can feel what's happening (which he probably can't), he can't control the leakage. See your pediatrician to discuss the matter. If your son is in fact encopretic, he may need a stool softener or enema until he can pass the mass, and a better diet (more vegetables, whole grains, fruit, and water) to prevent a recurrence. Once his bowel movements are back to normal, it may take a while to get him to have bowel movements in the potty again. Have him sit on it five to ten minutes around the time you expect him to have a bowel movement. Put him back in a diaper if he doesn't have one in the potty, and if he does, he can wear underpants.

Q: Is it really possible to train infants to use the potty? How?

• • •

A: Yes, it is absolutely possible. This more natural training method is gaining in popularity again since it is more hygienic and creates stronger parent-child bonds. The parent must remain attentive in order to recognize when the infant is about to urinate or have a bowel movement. While cradling the baby, the parent quickly places a pot under its bottom to "catch" the waste, and makes a special "ssss" or "shshsh" sound as the infant is relieving herself. If this is done consistently, the infant develops a conditioned response. Then, whenever she recognizes the sensation of the pot on her bottom and detects the special sound, she automatically pushes to relieve herself. If any waste is in the bowel or bladder, it will come out.

Parents can reduce or eliminate the need for diapers, and infants don't have to lie in their waste, though many parents do diaper their babies at night. Infants soon begin signaling for their little pot by fussing and reaching for it when they need to eliminate, just as they signal for a bottle when they want to be fed. The biggest problem is that few mentors are available to school new mothers in the art of infant training. See the Resources for recommended books.

Q: My toddler has asthma. Is it possible that he is allergic to a diapering product?

• • •

A: Some of the chemicals used to manufacture disposable diapers irritate the bronchial tubes and are known to produce asthma-like symptoms in susceptible youngsters. Children don't even have to be wearing a disposable diaper to become symptomatic—simply being in the same room with one can trigger an attack. The harsh liquids used to wash cloth diapers can be a real problem, too. Be sure to put them through an extra final rinse to remove chemical residues. Sometimes changing brands of disposable diapers or detergents can solve the problem. Instead of talcum powder, try cornstarch or plain flour (bake it first so it doesn't become gooey when wet). Otherwise, if you continue to suspect that a diapering product is endangering your child's health, begin potty training immediately.

Q: My two-year-old pees in the toilet, but absolutely will not poop in it. Instead, he goes in his bedroom when he thinks I'm not looking.

• • •

A: This is actually a very common problem, although that doesn't make it less difficult! Potty refusals often begin during a bout of constipation. Toddlers associate the pain of passing a hard movement with the potty, and become afraid to use it again. Or they get splashed with cold water when sitting on a potty seat on a regular toilet, and refuse to have any more bowel movements there. Many children are upset when they see their stool flushed away, as if part of themselves were disappearing down the drain. Others find standing or squatting a more comfortable position and have difficulty passing a bowel movement when sitting down.

Let your child wear regular underwear, and when you see signs that a bowel movement is starting, offer him a diaper. Stay close by so you can retrieve the dirty diaper afterward so he doesn't succumb to temptation and play with his B.M. Be careful he doesn't see you dispose of his diaper or its contents. Store the diaper in a lidded pail, and empty the pail when he's sleeping.

Q: My daughter trained easily, but I'm having trouble potty training my son. I've heard boys take longer to train than girls. Is it true?

• • •

A: On average, boys do finish training a few months later than girls. This difference may be due to the fact that boys mature a bit more slowly. Little boys tend to be more active and less compliant than girls, too, which makes training more difficult. However, younger siblings typically train sooner because they want to mimic their big brother or sister.

Be patient with your little guy, and try not to compare your children. Each one is different, with a unique personality and rate of development. Holding one sibling to the standards of the other erodes self-esteem and can translate into more intense sibling rivalry. What worked for your daughter may not work for your son, so check out several methods before deciding how to proceed.

Q: My last attempt at potty training my daughter ended up being a miserable experience for both of us. Now she won't even go near the potty. Where do I go from here?

• • •

A: Put her back in diapers, put the potty away, and give her a month to forget. Then, start reintroducing the potty very gradually. Put it in her play area so she can see it for a few days. Then invite her to sit on it fully clothed while you read her a story. Have her accompany you to the bathroom or leave the door open so she can watch you use the toilet. Ask her to hand you toilet paper and help you flush. A few days later, put her potty in the bathroom and suggest she feed a doll a bottle and have the doll use the potty while you use the toilet. Next, suggest she sit on the potty chair in the bathroom while you read her a story. After a few days of story reading, see if she will sit on her potty with nothing on her bottom. Tell her she is "just like Mama." Thereafter, see if you can get her to sit on the potty once a day without anything on her bottom, timing it so she might use it, and praising her if she succeeds. Whatever you do, avoid chastising her for accidents. Instead, try a reward system.

Q: Does the way toddlers are potty trained form their personalities?

• • •

A: Actually, it's more likely that children's personalities will dictate how easy or difficult they are to potty train. Easygoing youngsters with regular systems who adapt well to change are usually easiest to train. Shy youngsters are often more fearful of the potty at the outset and have bigger setbacks if something scares them during training. Insecure youngsters can become overwhelmed by the challenge if the pace of potty training is too fast, and are more inclined to give up after they've been criticized for an accident. More active children will have a harder time sitting still, which makes them more difficult to train. Parents have a harder time helping an irregular child get to the potty at the right time, which makes it harder for them to learn the process.

Certainly, abusing children during potty training warps their personality development, and shaming and humiliating them erodes their self-esteem. Harsh criticism can upset an overly sensitive tyke enough to cause posttraumatic stress syndrome, which creates serious emotional difficulties. Barring something so drastic, potty training doesn't have much, if anything, to do with personality development. Parents have less of a hand in molding their children than people generally think!

Q: **What rewards work best for toddlers?**

• • •

A: It really depends on the toddler. A smile and approving nod is all the reward many youngsters need. However, during the oppositional two-year-old stage, children are often driven to do the opposite of whatever they think parents want them to do, so parental praise may backfire. A spray of perfume and the statement, "You smell as pretty as a flower now that you used the potty instead of wetting your diapers," delights little boys as well as little girls. Stickers and the chance to wear real underwear are very popular, but some toddlers soon lose interest. The chance to earn a Hot Wheels toy has induced lots of toddler boys to drop everything and run to the potty time and again. The opportunity to do something special such as paint or blow bubbles works for many toddlers, but to be effective, rewards must be given immediately after a potty success. Lots of parents find that an M&M, animal cracker, or piece of sweetened cereal works better than anything else. Remember that rewards can be given for any "success," including just sitting on the potty.

Q: My child hasn't had an accident during the day for six months, but he still wets the bed at night. Is this normal?

• • •

A: Although there are no hard and fast rules, children typically start staying dry at night around the same time they are using the potty regularly during the day. Children with a relative who wet the bed as a youngster are at greater risk for bedwetting; boys are more often bedwetters than girls; and anxiety and depression can cause temporary bouts of bedwetting, too. Eventually, however, most children simply outgrow it.

Treatments aren't available until age five, so about the only solution is to try to cut down on the number of accidents by limiting fluids in the evening and taking him to the potty during the night. Put your child to bed in a diaper and use a waterproof pad to protect the mattress. If you can determine when the wetting usually happens and carry him to the potty before then, you may prevent it. After being taken regularly during the night for a time, some children stop bedwetting.

Whatever you do, don't get angry. Bedwetting isn't something children can control. Since anxiety and depression can also cause bedwetting, punishments can make things worse.

Q: My thirty-month-old is so defiant, I've been dreading trying to potty train him. My mother has offered to give it a try. I'm wondering if I should let her.

• • •

A: Because toddlers are trying to establish a separate identity, they usually save their worst behavior for the people they are closest to. Your son may in fact respond better to someone with whom he has a less intense relationship, assuming that it is a good one. Toddlers are often "trained" to use the potty by day care friends and older siblings.

Talk to your mother first, to be sure you are comfortable with the methods she plans to use. You must be able to support her efforts by using the same methods in your home.

Arrange the schedule so that your son returns home each evening. Potty training is stressful because children are excited, are learning so many new things at once, and must really concentrate. Unless your youngster is accustomed to being with his grandmother for extended periods, a bout of homesickness could end up making it harder for him to give potty training his all.

APPENDIX B

Chart Your Progress

Photocopy or cut out this reward chart, post it near the potty, and affix stars or draw smiley faces to record your child's potty successes. The chance to earn stickers and stars serves as an incentive, and the display of past victories can encourage your child after an accident.

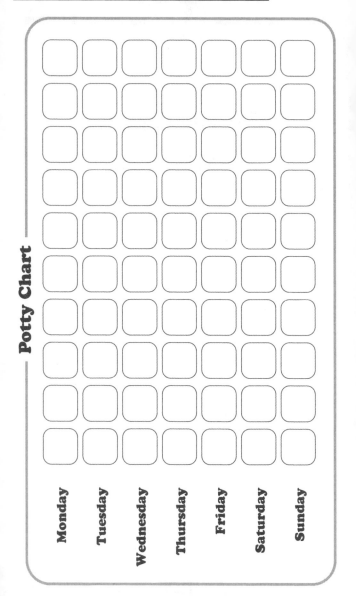

Potty Chart

Monday
Tuesday
Wednesday
Thursday
Friday
Saturday
Sunday

Resources

As you prepare for training your child—or continue your ongoing efforts—you'll find a variety of resources for adults and children. Parenting books, videos, and Web sites are all excellent sources of information. Remember, however, that if you have concerns regarding your child's health or well-being, you should call your pediatrician.

Children's Books

Sanschagrin, Joceline, and Helene Desputeaux. *Caillou-Potty Time* (Chouette Publishing, 2000). If your toddler's PBS hero can do it, so can your toddler.

....

Mack, Allison. *Dry All Night* (Little, Brown, & Company, 1989). For parents (Part 1) and for older children who can read (Part 2), this book is definitely worth a look-see if bedwetting is hampering your youngster's social life.

....

Gomi, Taro, and Amanda Mayer Stinchecum. *Everybody Poops* (Kane/Miller Publisher, 1993). This book explains elimination in terms a little one can understand.

....

Worth, Bonnie, and David Prebenna (illustrator). *I Can Go Potty* (Bonnie Worth, 1999). If your child's old hero, Kermit, can do it, so can your child.

....

Cole, Joanna, and Maxie Chambliss. *My Big Boy Potty* and *My Big Girl Potty*. (HarperCollins Juvenile Books, 2000). The text reassures little ones that practice makes perfect and gives the impression that anyone can accomplish this feat.

....

Frankel, Alona. *Once Upon a Potty* (HarperCollins Juvenile Books, 1999). Available in boy and girl formats and packaged with a doll, this book can be used to introduce babies and toddlers to a new potty, but even three-year-olds find the messages about accidents reassuring.

Capucilli, Alissa S., and Dorothy Stott (illustrator). *The Potty Book for Boys* (Barrons Educational Series, 2000). A rhyming book.

Lewison, Wendy. *The Princess and the Potty* (Aladdin Paperbacks, 1998). The princess breaks down and uses the potty so as not to wet her darling pantaloons.

McGrath, Bob, and Shelley Dieterichs (illustrator). *Uh Oh! Gotta Go!* (Barrons Juveniles, 1996). Yet another good one.

Borgardt, Marianne, and Maxie Chambliss (illustrator). *What Do You Do with a Potty?: An Important Pop-up Book* (Golden Books, 1994). Your child can pull, lift, and learn.

Murkoff, Heidi, and Laura Rader (illustrator). *What to Expect When You Use the Potty* (HarperCollins Juvenile Books, 2000). Another good one to add to your child's collection.

Kriegman, Janelle, Mitchell Kriegman, and Kathryn Mitter (illustrator). *When You've Got to Go!* (Bear in the Big Blue House) (Simon Spotlight, 2000). This one is sure to drum up some enthusiasm for potty training—it comes packaged with the video, *Bear in the Big Blue*

House—Potty Time with Bear (1997) by Mitchell Kriegman and Richard A. Fernandes, directors.

Cole, Joanna, with photos by Margaret Miller. *Your New Potty* (Morrow Junior Books, 1989). The introduction contains guidelines for parents.

Potty Training Books for Parents

Boucke, Laurie. *Infant Potty Training* (White-Boucke Publishing, 2002). If you don't believe infant potty training is the gentler, more natural way before you read this comprehensive tome on the subject, you will afterward!

Faull, Jan. *Mommy I Have to Go Potty: A Parent's Guide to Toilet Training* (Parenting Press, 1996). A potties-without-pressure approach for older toddlers who are self-motivated.

VanPelt, Katie. *Potty Training Your Baby* (Avery Publishing Group, 1996). Start early on, after youngsters can sit up and long before the terribly trying twos begin, and potty training is likely to be much easier.

Azrin, Nathan H., and Richard M. Foxx. *Toilet Training in a Day* (Pocket Books, 1974). A step-by-step guide to putting children age two and over on the fast track to speed learning.

Schaefer, Charles E., and Theresa Foy DiGeronimo. *Toilet Training Without Tears* (Signet Penguin Group, 1997). Learn to set loving limits, and read about the special techniques for training children with developmental delays.

Boucke, Laurie. *Trickle Treat: Diaperless Infant Toilet Training Method* (White-Boucke Publishing, 1991). All the basic how-to info you need to get started!

Technical Journal Articles

"Diagnosis and Treatment for Children Who Cannot Control Urination." Max Maizels, Kevin Gandhi, Barbara Keating, and Diane Rosenblum. *Current Problems in Pediatrics*, November/December, 1993 (pages 402–450). If your child's pediatrician isn't knowledgeable about all of the organic problems and treatments for uncontrolled wetting—and many are not—this article can fill that gap.

Professional Help

National Enuresis Society (NES). A not-for-profit organization of doctors, medical personnel, and other persons dedicated to building greater awareness and understanding of enuresis. *www.peds.umn.edu/Centers/NES/*

National Kidney Foundation (NKF) Supports children with bedwetting problems and their families, and provides information to professionals. Call 1-888-WAKE-DRY or see *www.bedwetting-nkfonline.org*.

Try for Dry. Get products for help diagnosing and treating bedwetting from the company that trains the docs! Call ☎ 773-989-1960, see 🖥 *www.tryfordry.com*, or e-mail *info@tryfordry.com*.

Online Resources

🖥 *www.babyminestore.com*. Baby-friendly diapers, diaper covers, training pants, potty seats, and more. Phone ☎ 623-974-4457 for a catalog.

....

🖥 *www.babyparenting.about.com*. Potty training tips and the chance to network with other online parents are a click away.

....

🖥 *www.drsonna.org*. Receive a personal reply to your potty training questions from the author.

....

🖥 *www.parents-choice.org*. Lists the books, toys, videos, and software that other parents have given a thumbs-up.

....

🖥 *www.pottytrainingsolutions.com*. The one-stop Web site for training products, books, tapes, even homeopathic remedies. Call ☎ 480-883-9765 for a catalog.

....

🖥 *www.pottypaper.com*. Specially designed toilet paper and toilet seats shaped like ducks will enchant your child. The portable potty chair shaped like a car will increase your child's motivation to use the potty while traveling.

✑ *www.tnpc.com.* Research before you buy a potty chair by checking recommendations and recalls at the National Parenting Center's Seal of Approval Web site.

✑ *www.weebees.com.* Find the hard-to-find earth-friendly diapering and training products.

✑ *www.White-Boucke.com.* Laurie Boucke's infant potty training center.

General Parenting Books

Sonna, Linda. *The Everything® Toddler Book* (Adams Media Corporation, 2002).

Brazelton, T. Berry. *Touchpoints, The Essential Reference: Your Child's Emotional and Behavioral Development* (Addison-Wesley Publishing Company, 1992).

Eisenberg, Arlene, Sandee E. Hathaway, and Heidi E. Murkoff. *What to Expect During the Toddler Years* (Workman Publishing, 1996).

Index

We Have EVERYTHING!

BUSINESS

Everything® **Business Planning Book**
Everything® **Coaching and Mentoring Book**
Everything® **Fundraising Book**
Everything® **Home-Based Business Book**
Everything® **Leadership Book**
Everything® **Managing People Book**
Everything® **Network Marketing Book**
Everything® **Online Business Book**
Everything® **Project Management Book**
Everything® **Selling Book**
Everything® **Start Your Own Business Book**
Everything® **Time Management Book**

COMPUTERS

Everything® **Build Your Own Home Page Book**
Everything® **Computer Book**
Everything® **Internet Book**
Everything® **Microsoft® Word 2000 Book**

COOKBOOKS

Everything® **Barbecue Cookbook**
Everything® **Bartender's Book, $9.95**
Everything® **Chinese Cookbook**
Everything® **Chocolate Cookbook**
Everything® **Cookbook**
Everything® **Dessert Cookbook**
Everything® **Diabetes Cookbook**
Everything® **Low-Carb Cookbook**
Everything® **Low-Fat High-Flavor Cookbook**
Everything® **Mediterranean Cookbook**
Everything® **Mexican Cookbook**
Everything® **One-Pot Cookbook**
Everything® **Pasta Book**
Everything® **Quick Meals Cookbook**
Everything® **Slow Cooker Cookbook**
Everything® **Soup Cookbook**
Everything® **Thai Cookbook**
Everything® **Vegetarian Cookbook**
Everything® **Wine Book**

HEALTH

Everything® **Anti-Aging Book**
Everything® **Diabetes Book**
Everything® **Dieting Book**
Everything® **Herbal Remedies Book**
Everything® **Hypnosis Book**
Everything® **Menopause Book**
Everything® **Nutrition Book**
Everything® **Reflexology Book**
Everything® **Stress Management Book**
Everything® **Vitamins, Minerals, and Nutritional Supplements Book**

HISTORY

Everything® **American History Book**
Everything® **Civil War Book**
Everything® **Irish History & Heritage Book**
Everything® **Mafia Book**
Everything® **World War II Book**

HOBBIES & GAMES

Everything® **Bridge Book**
Everything® **Candlemaking Book**
Everything® **Casino Gambling Book**
Everything® **Chess Basics Book**
Everything® **Collectibles Book**
Everything® **Crossword and Puzzle Book**
Everything® **Digital Photography Book**
Everything® **Family Tree Book**
Everything® **Games Book**
Everything® **Knitting Book**
Everything® **Magic Book**
Everything® **Motorcycle Book**
Everything® **Online Genealogy Book**
Everything® **Photography Book**
Everything® **Pool & Billiards Book**
Everything® **Quilting Book**
Everything® **Scrapbooking Book**
Everything® **Soapmaking Book**

HOME IMPROVEMENT

Everything® **Feng Shui Book**
Everything® **Gardening Book**
Everything® **Home Decorating Book**
Everything® **Landscaping Book**
Everything® **Lawn Care Book**
Everything® **Organize Your Home Book**

KIDS' STORY BOOKS

Everything® **Bedtime Story Book**
Everything® **Bible Stories Book**
Everything® **Fairy Tales Book**
Everything® **Mother Goose Book**

LANGUAGE

Everything® **Learning French Book**

Everything® **Learning German Book**

Everything® **Learning Italian Book**

Everything® **Learning Latin Book**

Everything® **Learning Spanish Book**

Everything® **Sign Language Book**

MUSIC

Everything® **Drums Book (with CD), $19.95 ($31.95 CAN)**

Everything® **Guitar Book**

Everything® **Playing Piano and Keyboards Book**

Everything® **Rock & Blues Guitar Book (with CD), $19.95 ($31.95 CAN)**

Everything® **Songwriting Book**

NEW AGE

Everything® **Astrology Book**

Everything® **Divining the Future Book**

Everything® **Dreams Book**

Everything® **Ghost Book**

Everything® **Meditation Book**

Everything® **Numerology Book**

Everything® **Palmistry Book**

Everything® **Psychic Book**

Everything® **Spells & Charms Book**

Everything® **Tarot Book**

Everything® **Wicca and Witchcraft Book**

PARENTING

Everything® **Baby Names Book**

Everything® **Baby Shower Book**

Everything® **Baby's First Food Book**

Everything® **Baby's First Year Book**

Everything® **Breastfeeding Book**

Everything® **Father-to-Be Book**

Everything® **Get Ready for Baby Book**

Everything® **Home-schooling Book**

Everything® **Parent's Guide to Positive Discipline**

Everything® **Potty Training Book, $9.95 ($15.95 CAN)**

Everything® **Pregnancy Book, 2nd Ed.**

Everything® **Pregnancy Fitness Book**

Everything® **Pregnancy Organizer, $15.00 ($22.95 CAN)**

Everything® **Toddler Book**

Everything® **Tween Book**

PERSONAL FINANCE

Everything® **Budgeting Book**

Everything® **Get Out of Debt Book**

Everything® **Get Rich Book**

Everything® **Homebuying Book, 2nd Ed.**

Everything® **Homeselling Book**

Everything® **Investing Book**

Everything® **Money Book**

Everything® **Mutual Funds Book**

Everything® **Online Investing Book**

Everything® **Personal Finance Book**

Everything® **Personal Finance in Your 20s & 30s Book**

Everything® **Wills & Estate Planning Book**

PETS

Everything® **Cat Book**

Everything® **Dog Book**

Everything® **Dog Training and Tricks Book**

Everything® **Horse Book**

Everything® **Puppy Book**

Everything® **Tropical Fish Book**

REFERENCE

Everything® **Astronomy Book**

Everything® **Car Care Book**

Everything® **Christmas Book, $15.00 ($21.95 CAN)**

Everything® **Classical Mythology Book**

Everything® **Einstein Book**

Everything® **Etiquette Book**

Everything® **Great Thinkers Book**

Everything® **Philosophy Book**

Everything® **Shakespeare Book**

Everything® **Tall Tales, Legends, & Other Outrageous Lies Book**

Everything® **Toasts Book**

Everything® **Trivia Book**

Everything® **Weather Book**

RELIGION

Everything® **Angels Book**

Everything® **Buddhism Book**

Everything® **Catholicism Book**

Everything® **Jewish History & Heritage Book**

Everything® **Judaism Book**

Everything® **Prayer Book**

Everything® **Saints Book**

Everything® **Understanding Islam Book**

Everything® **World's Religions Book**

Everything® **Zen Book**

SCHOOL & CAREERS

Everything® **After College Book**

Everything® **College Survival Book**

Everything® **Cover Letter Book**

Everything® **Get-a-Job Book**

Everything® **Hot Careers Book**

Everything® **Job Interview Book**

Everything® **Online Job Search Book**

Everything® **Resume Book, 2nd Ed.**

Everything® **Study Book**

SELF-HELP

Everything® Dating Book
Everything® Divorce Book
Everything® Great Marriage Book
Everything® Great Sex Book
Everything® Romance Book
Everything® Self-Esteem Book
Everything® Success Book

SPORTS & FITNESS

Everything® Bicycle Book
Everything® Body Shaping Book
Everything® Fishing Book
Everything® Fly-Fishing Book
Everything® Golf Book
Everything® Golf Instruction Book
Everything® Pilates Book
Everything® Running Book
Everything® Sailing Book, 2nd Ed.
Everything® T'ai Chi and QiGong Book
Everything® Total Fitness Book
Everything® Weight Training Book
Everything® Yoga Book

TRAVEL

Everything® Guide to Las Vegas
Everything® Guide to New England
Everything® Guide to New York City
Everything® Guide to Washington D.C.
Everything® Travel Guide to The Disneyland Resort®, California Adventure®, Universal Studios®, and the Anaheim Area

Everything® Travel Guide to the Walt Disney World Resort®, Universal Studios®, and Greater Orlando, 3rd Ed.

WEDDINGS

Everything® Bachelorette Party Book
Everything® Bridesmaid Book
Everything® Creative Wedding Ideas Book
Everything® Jewish Wedding Book
Everything® Wedding Book, 2nd Ed.
Everything® Wedding Checklist, $7.95 ($11.95 CAN)
Everything® Wedding Etiquette Book, $7.95 ($11.95 CAN)
Everything® Wedding Organizer, $15.00 ($22.95 CAN)
Everything® Wedding Shower Book, $7.95 ($12.95 CAN)
Everything® Wedding Vows Book, $7.95 ($11.95 CAN)
Everything® Weddings on a Budget Book, $9.95 ($15.95 CAN)

WRITING

Everything® Creative Writing Book
Everything® Get Published Book
Everything® Grammar and Style Book
Everything® Grant Writing Book

Everything® Guide to Writing Children's Books
Everything® Screenwriting Book
Everything® Writing Well Book

EVERYTHING® KIDS' BOOKS

All titles are $6.95 and $10.95 CAN (unless otherwise noted)

Everything® Kids' Baseball Book, 2nd Ed.
Everything® Kids' Bugs Book
Everything® Kids' Christmas Puzzle & Activity Book
Everything® Kids' Cookbook
Everything® Kids' Halloween Puzzle & Activity Book
Everything® Kids' Joke Book
Everything® Kids' Math Puzzles Book
Everything® Kids' Mazes Book
Everything® Kids' Money Book ($11.95 CAN)
Everything® Kids' Monsters Book
Everything® Kids' Nature Book ($11.95 CAN)
Everything® Kids' Puzzle Book
Everything® Kids' Science Experiments Book
Everything® Kids' Soccer Book
Everything® Kids' Travel Activity Book

All Everything® books are priced at $12.95 or $14.95, unless otherwise stated.
Prices subject to change without notice.
Canadian prices range from $11.95–$31.95, and are subject to change without notice.